THE QUILT DIGEST

THE QUILT DIGEST PRESS
SAN FRANCISCO
5

❦

To the memory of
Edwin Binney, 3rd
Collector, intellectual and friend

ISBN 0-913327-13-1
ISSN 0740-4093
Library of Congress Catalog Card Number: 82-90743

Edited by Michael M. Kile.
Book design by Patricia Koren and Laurie Smith, Kajun Graphics, San Francisco.
Editing assistance provided by Harold Nadel, San Francisco.
Typographical composition in Sabon by Rock & Jones, Oakland, California.
Color photographs not specifically credited were taken by Sharon Risedorph,
San Francisco.
Printed on 100 lb. Satin Kinfuji and 260g/m² Bon Ivory (cover) by
Nissha Printing Company, Ltd., Kyoto, Japan.
Color separations by the printer.

First printing.

The Quilt Digest Press
955 Fourteenth Street
San Francisco 94114

CONTENTS

❦

Fragile Families: Quilts as Kinship Bonds
by Ricky Clark

A remarkable illumination of how quilts unite the generations.

❦

Pieces of the Heart
by Mary Coyne Penders

A sensitive portrait of six international quiltmakers.

❦

Showcase
Compiled by Roderick Kiracofe

Our fifth-anniversary selection of fine antique and contemporary
quilts from across the country and around the world.

❦

When the Smoke Cleared
by Dorothy Cozart

An intriguing exploration of unusual, often zany, antique quilts
made from fabrics issued by cigar and cigarette manufacturers.

❦

Quilts and Their Makers
in Nineteenth-Century Australia
by Annette Gero

The first comprehensive presentation of Australia's rich
quilt heritage.

❦

The Collector: Something Old, Something New
by Michael Kile

A trailblazing couple's collection of not only fine antique quilts
but contemporary masterpieces as well.

A c. 1893 photograph of Pauline Cawker (top), her daughter Hortense and sister Leonore.
Photograph courtesy of Peter C. Merrill, a grandson of Pauline Cawker.

Fragile Families
Quilts as Kinship Bonds

THE TEXT read like a legal brief: solemn, specific, formal. It might have been inscribed in elegant Spencerian script on brittle parchment, rolled and tied with narrow red ribbon and discovered years later in the dusty pigeonhole of a roll-top desk.

But no bespectacled attorney had drafted this 1851 instrument. The penmanship was neat, but undistinguished. Brown ink had flowed from a rather worn nub onto an eight-inch square of ordinary white muslin. And small, neat stitches preserved this document in the center of the top row of blocks on a quilt that never saw the insides of a law office. The inscription read:

This quilt, commenced by our dear Laura & finished by me, principally from fragments of her dresses, I give & bequeath unto her sister Julia M. Woodruff, or in case of her death to her sister Hila M. Hall, if she survives, otherwise to the oldest surviving granddaughter of their father, Artemas Mahan deceased.
   Sarah Mahan.
   Oberlin Feb. 6, 1851.

For Sarah, widow of Artemas Mahan and loving stepmother of "our dear Laura" and her sisters, this quilt was a family bond that joined its members together more strongly than any legal document; and within that family, women constituted a special group. Sarah's quilt block occupied the same position on the quilt as the referenced women did in her life—top center. When Laura Mahan died, Sarah gathered the fragments of her stepdaughter's life and stitched them together to create a warming comforter. It was her way of coping with the pain incurred by a break in the family. By bequeathing the quilt first to Laura's sisters and then to their daughters, Sarah forged a chain of love and solidarity linking together three generations of women in the Mahan family.

A bequest inscribed on a quilt is rare. But Sarah's response is not. In nineteenth-century America, women often made quilts to preserve kinship ties and give assurances of steadfast affection when the family circle was broken.

BY RICKY CLARK

The basic word is "family." For Sarah Mahan and other women of the nineteenth century, family was the core of their universe, home the focus of their lives.

A century earlier the family had been the primary economic unit of American society. Men, women and even children contributed to the family's livelihood, and the contributions of each were recognized as valuable. But, with increased industrialization during the nineteenth century, the economic partnership of families was upset and the lives of men and women increasingly separated. For the first time, husbands left their homes to earn a living, and home management and child-rearing became the sole responsibility of their wives. Men and women saw their world divided into two gender-based "spheres," each encompassing different activities and espousing different values.

The world of commerce was considered the domain of men and the family circle was women's "peculiar sphere." Women were considered uniquely prepared to comfort their world-weary husbands and mold the characters of their children because they were believed to be instinctively pious, self-sacrificing and domestic.[1]

Described as "calculating" and "desolate of feeling," the pecuniary world of men was portrayed as a place in which "every principle of justice and honor, and even the dictates of common honesty [are] disregarded."[2] Fortunately, a husband could be restored in his home, "an elysium to which he can flee and find rest from the stormy strife of a selfish world."[3] The family, in fact, was considered "the one morally reliable institution in a fluid and diffuse society."[4] Men and women alike looked to the "sacred" and "hallowed" family—and especially to the pious wives and mothers who presided over it—for salvation from the exploitative values of the marketplace. They elevated the family to a position a little lower than the angels and crowned it with all the attributes usually ascribed to Heaven itself.

Encouraged by advice books, ministers and magazines, Americans revered "an influence...so silent and quiet, that it attracts but little notice, and yet so pervading that the whole body of society feels its transforming power. *It is Woman's influence in domestic life.* The hallowed names of Wife and Mother convey the meaning of it all."[5]

And by those hallowed names, and others that described women's relationships within the family, nineteenth-century women defined themselves. *Mother, daughter, sister, wife* appear repeatedly in published and private writings, institutional records, and on quilts and gravestones, usually preceded by effusive and complimentary adjectives.

But, in spite of the rhetoric, the world of nineteenth-century women was insecure. And they knew it. In this new industrial society, some men made fortunes and lost them overnight. Restless or adventurous husbands sought a better life in the undiscovered West, dragging reluctant wives and children behind them. Death was such a familiar visitor that many women discovered, as did Sarah Mahan, that marriage was but a brief episode in their difficult lives. When husbands died or deserted their families, women had little financial or legal protection.

Women found security in a family-based female world characterized by strong ties of mutual need and deep affection. Accepting domesticity as a womanly virtue, they broadened their definition of "family" to include an extensive network of female relatives, friends and women with whom they shared the religious and reform activities they saw as the logical extension of their

Ohio Star, begun by Laura Mahan, c. 1847, and completed by her stepmother Sarah Mahan in 1851, Oberlin, Ohio, 76 1/2 × 87 1/2 inches, pieced cottons, with ink inscriptions. Collection of the Allen Memorial Art Museum, Oberlin, Ohio, accession no. 85.24, Special Acquisitions Fund and gift of private donors.

duties as protectors of the home. They worked together in church sewing societies, stitching garments for destitute women and children, and in female reform societies fighting slavery, alcohol and other social evils that destroyed the sacred family circle. These bonds were so strong, supportive and long-lasting that women compared them to the family relationships they most resembled—sisterhood.[6]

Ties to their sisters in this enlarged family provided stability in a hostile and threatening world, and such bonds were life-long. Even after they married, women continued to fulfill their duties as daughters and sisters, helping each other in times of illness and childbirth, providing financial aid when possible and raising each other's children in cases of death.

When families were broken, as inevitably they were, women strove to preserve their ties of love and support. They visited each other, often for months at a time. They corresponded regularly and exchanged diaries kept just for that purpose. "I find I cannot live without writing everything to you," Laura Clark confided to her mother shortly after emigrating from Connecticut to Ohio in 1818. "How much I would give to be there ... [and] to enjoy the blessed company of my most dear friends."[7] Sarah Mahan's young Oberlin neighbor Helen Cowles lived for letters from home during the winter she taught in Cincinnati: "When shall I hear from you again?" she implored her parents. "I cannot wait long. O I cannot! Your letters always encourage me to go on and do good. I feast on them.... Let me have some more letters soon."[8] Exchanging miniature portraits or daguerreotypes became a stan-

dard part of preparing for departure. Catharine Beecher, a champion of women's domestic education, wrote of her preparations for a trip in 1848: "I made my will, had my daguerreotype taken for father, and made all other proper arrangements for a roll down the Alleghenies."[9]

But more durable than letters and more nurturing than daguerreotypes were the quilts women made to bridge gaps in the family circle. Some they gave to wives of restless husbands infected with "land fever," as warm assurances of continued affection. Others were made, as Sarah Mahan's was, to keep alive a family relationship broken by death. For women whose lives had been so intertwined, these tactile, familiar reminders of home and shared domestic work became symbols of the strong and loving ties that underlay women's family relationships. They were truly comforters.

*M*ary Tolford must have needed comforting when she left Sherbrooke, Quebec, in 1845 with her husband and three little girls. Her home had always been in the Northeast, and now she was leaving for distant Ohio.

Mary was born in Harvard, Massachusetts, in 1808, but by the time she married Calvin Tolford in 1831 she was living in Concord, New Hampshire. Calvin Tolford, although a fourth-generation New Englander, was not content to stay in New Hampshire, however, and after their marriage took Mary to Sherbrooke, where he edited a weekly newspaper, *The St. Francis Courier.* A son, John, who died in in-

fancy, and two daughters, Mary and Adeline, were born in Canada. Sherbrooke was close enough to Concord for Mary to take her children back for visits often. In 1838, when she was again pregnant, she turned to the women in her family, as did so many nineteenth-century women, and her third daughter, Julia, was born in Concord.

Mary's attachment to her Concord sisterhood was strong. Relatives and friends alike had rejoiced with her when she married, grieved with her at the death of her son, and nursed her through Julia's birth. Their friendship had continued even after her move to Canada, and was sustained by her periodic visits. But in 1845 the Tolfords moved again, and this time their new home was much farther away—in Marietta, Ohio.

The experience of leaving home during the period of westward expansion was anguishing for women. Many accompanied their husbands from a sense of obligation rather than a shared desire for adventure, and both the women who left and those in their families who stayed behind dreaded such occasions. When they finally parted, they knew this separation might well be permanent. All families had suffered the deaths of loved ones, and the undiscovered West presented new and unknown threats.

Her friends knew they might never see Mary again. Wanting to comfort her and to assure her of their affection, they made a quilt for her and inscribed it with uplifting Bible verses and loving sentiments. The *Album Patch* pattern they chose was a favorite among New England women, who saw so many sisters depart for the West.[10]

Signature quilts were textile

Album Patch, *by friends of Mary Pollard Tolford, Concord, New Hampshire,*
1844–1845, 83 1/2 × 77 inches, pieced cottons, with ink inscriptions.
Collection of Betty Clements, a great-granddaughter of Mary Pollard Tolford.

versions of the autograph albums popular at the same time; both served as tangible links to absent sisters. It is hardly coincidental that so many signature quilts were made during the period of westward expansion; in fact, a recent study reports a high correlation between domestic dislocation and the making of signature quilts during the mid-nineteenth century.[11] This restless, mobile era was the time when women most needed to affirm strong family bonds.

The inscriptions on Mary Tolford's quilt, like those on so many others made for women emigrating to the unknown West, are touching testimonies to life-long affection and the pain of separation. Some blocks are signed "your friend," others "Sister." In this age of strong, family-based female networks, the distinction between chosen friends and kin was blurred and the terms often used interchangeably.[12]

The most poignant inscriptions on Mary's quilt are solemn assurances of continuing love and support and hopes of being remembered. Maria Millard expected Mary to read the inscriptions frequently and assumed they would evoke fond memories of her friends, even as she made new ones:

As often as you look this bedquilt over
And over beloved names you sigh
And others may delight you more
May mine not pass unheeded by.

The quiltmakers' fears of being forgotten were unwarranted. Mary cherished her quilt, and when her oldest daughter, her namesake, left home to teach, it was presented to her.

Young Mary Tolford had been eleven when her mother's quilt was made, and probably knew the women who signed it. Most were friends living in Concord; others, such as "Your little cousins/Mary Amanda Webster/Lucilla Webster," were relatives. Through this quilt, young Mary's ties to New England were kept alive.

She might have needed such bonds more than most; the Tolfords moved frequently. By the time she was twenty-three, young Mary Tolford had lived in Quebec, Ohio, Kentucky and Illinois.

Born in Canada in 1834, Mary lived with her parents and sisters until 1855, when she left their Marietta home to teach first in Laurel Furnace, Kentucky, and then in Monmouth, Illinois. In Monmouth, Mary not only found a new job, but also established a new home. She married Abner Page, the widowed father of six, and over the years she and Abner added nine more children to the family.

Mary brought to Monmouth two tangible ties to her earlier life: her mother's quilt, signed by family and friends in New Hampshire, and an autograph album signed by her two sisters and friends in Ohio and Kentucky. The cover of Mary's album, with its image of a bereaved woman winding garlands around a tomb, tellingly portrays the pain of dislocation by comparing it to the final separation of death. The sentiments recorded in the album support this, and are similar to those on her quilt:

While tossed upon life's surging waves,
That never ceasing, rise and fall,
Continual partings, friend from friend,
Must be the certain lot of all.[13]

Continual partings from friends had taken their toll, and Mary was content to spend the rest of her life in Monmouth. During her first year there she confided to her diary:

Mother writes me that they are going to move again, which I am very sorry to hear on her account. Wonder if the time will ever come when my Father will be settled in a home, a real home![14]

Mary Tolford left home for the first time to teach in a school, but many nineteenth-century girls left home for the first time to attend one. Their future roles as wives and mothers were considered important enough to warrant thorough and structured training. Throughout the century, academies and "female seminaries" grew like mushrooms. All accepted local students, and some had boarding students as well. Many schools were organized and governed like families; even the language used in such schools was familial.[15]

Students living away from home for the first time naturally missed their families, and some addressed this loss by organizing "Bands of Sisters" as soon as they arrived.[16] Many schools eased the transition for homesick young women: "matrons" who housed students at the Oberlin Collegiate Institute during the 1850's were advised to "exercise over all those connected with our family circle, as boarders, a maternal care, and watchfulness by trying to make the home circle pleasant and at-

Mary Tolford's autograph album. Collection of Betty Clements.

tractive," and to offer to students the same "privileges and . . . means of moral and mental improvement . . . as we would have furnished to our own daughters were they left to the mercy of a cold world."[17]

But not all students at female seminaries required the maternal care and watchfulness of surrogate parents. When Pauline Cawker attended Milwaukee College in the 1880's, she lived at home with her parents and younger sister, Leonore. Milwaukee College was then a private girls' school. Thirty years earlier this had been the last "female seminary" to attract the support of noted writer and educator Catharine Beecher, who crusaded tirelessly for schools to train women as homemakers and teachers. Her concerns for women extended to their working spaces, and the building which housed Milwaukee College when Pauline Cawker was there had been designed by the enterprising Miss Beecher.[18]

In October 1888, a month before her eighteenth birthday,

Pauline left Milwaukee College to be married. That same year her school friends made a quilt for her. Whether they knew of her wedding plans the previous December when "Jennie" embroidered the earliest date on Pauline's quilt can only be guessed. However, for nineteenth-century women, leaving the "band of sisters" at school was often as difficult as leaving the homes of their childhood. Many women also faced marriage with trepidation, even when those marriages were subsequently happy.[19] If the feelings of Pauline's friends were similar to her family's, she was sorely missed. "We began to think you had forgotten us," her father wrote only two days after her wedding. "Poor Leo [Leonore] went to bed crying. . . . Your mama seems to miss you very, very much."[20]

Pauline's friends made her a crazy quilt, typical of the era, but with a difference. They put a photograph of Pauline right in the center.

Pauline was a young woman with a thirst for adventure. Although she kept her home base in Milwaukee, she traveled widely all her life and described those trips vividly in letters to her daughter, Hortense. On one excursion she visited thirty cities in Europe and the Middle East, saw the Paris Exposition and an eruption of Mount Vesuvius, and witnessed an awesome parade escorting a sultan to prayers in Constantinople. "Never in my life have I witnessed such a ceremony," she wrote to Hortense in a colorful letter that brought to life white horses, uniformed troops, splendid carriages and exotic royalty.[21] In spite of a glamorous and adventurous life, however, the quilt made for her by her school friends evidently meant a great deal to Pauline, for she kept this symbol of sisterhood throughout her long life.

$\mathcal{S}$ix years after Pauline Cawker married, another bride left her childhood home. Cora Weeden grew up in Columbia, Ohio, the first town established in Lorain County. The community had been transplanted from Connecticut in 1807, when the entire Ohio tract was sold to a group of relatives and friends in Waterbury, Connecticut. Most of the original settlers remained in Columbia and their descendants still lived there in 1893, when Cora Weeden married Charles Mills.

Cora's mother, Margaret, must have missed her daughter as keenly as did Sarah Cawker after her daughter Pauline's wedding. The first year after Cora's marriage, Margaret made a quilt for her. It may have been a Christmas gift; one block includes the date "Dec. 25, 1894." Christmas was a special time for Margaret Weeden, whose own wedding had taken place less than a week before Christmas.

Margaret Weeden was an expert seamstress and a prolific quiltmaker, and it is hardly sur-

Crazy, *by friends of Pauline Adela Cawker, Milwaukee, Wisconsin, 1887–1888, 81 × 80 ½ inches, silks, satins and velvets, with paint and three-dimensional projections. Techniques include embroidery and photographic transfer. Collection of Ausma E. Merrill, the wife of Peter C. Merrill, a grandson of Pauline Adela Cawker.*

prising that she made a quilt for Cora, who didn't sew at all. But this quilt was not simply utilitarian. For Margaret, and for her daughter who kept the quilt all her life, it was a loving symbol of kinship, a way of affirming the strong family ties that existed in this close-knit community. Of the thirty-two names on the quilt, twelve are relatives, and some families are represented by as many as five signatures. The names of six ancestors, long dead, are inscribed on the quilt, as are the name and death date of Cora's sister, Minna, who had died fourteen years earlier. To Margaret Weeden, her deceased daughter was still a member of the family. The quilt, in fact, is a genealogical history of Margaret's family, traced back to its earliest settlers in Columbia.

Names on the Mahan, Tolford and Cawker quilts were apparently all of living people. But, to Margaret Weeden, "family" included ancestors as well as living relatives and friends. Including the names of deceased family members on a quilt was not uncommon in the nineteenth century. Many quilt blocks include birth and death dates as well as names. They read like tombstones, and in some respects they are.

Nineteenth-century Americans were obsessed with death. It was, of course, the ultimate break in the family circle, and anticipation of death was a major part of the apprehension women felt as they saw their sisters depart for the West. Just as relatives and friends absent because of westward migration were still considered family, so were the dead. The

Chimney Sweep *in a* Garden Maze, *by Margaret Weeden, Columbia, Ohio, c. 1894, 101 ½ × 81 ½ inches, pieced cottons, with ink inscriptions. Collection of Lorain County Historical Society, Elyria, Ohio, accession no.* K 49.

family was considered eternal, and since all family members would eventually die, no matter how far apart their homes on earth, Heaven was seen as the place where families separated by death would one day be restored.

As the family would be reunited spiritually after death, so it was reunited physically within family plots in cemeteries. It was important to families that their dead be returned even from the distant West for burial, so that they would not "rest all alone with strangers."[22] The "rural" or "garden" cemetery, so familiar to us today, was a greatly admired nineteenth-century creation. Boston's Mount Auburn Cemetery was described as "a vast and exquisitely beautiful dormitory," a "refuge" that could draw its visitors from "the busy competition and hurried . . . ambitious spirit of

the day."[23] It was, in other words, home.

Cemeteries spanned the chasm between bereaved families and their dead. So, too, did the posthumous portraits, photographs and hair ornaments treasured by survivors. And so did quilts. When families were broken by death, women used these tactile, homey comforters to preserve ties to their deceased loved ones.

Elizabeth Mitchell of Lewis County, Kentucky, recreated a rural cemetery in the center of the quilt she made in 1839, only eight years after Boston's Mount Auburn was created.[24] It portrays the Mitchell family plot, and the appliquéd coffins within it and along the outer border of the quilt are labeled with family names. Mrs. Mitchell moved these coffins from the world of the living, represented by the border, into the

cemetery as her relatives died. This domestic textile, much used, was the quiltmaker's bridge to her two sons and other deceased relatives. She used coffins to symbolize both the living and the dead because there was no lasting difference between them, and moved easily between the two worlds simply by relocating the coffins. By sleeping under this family comforter, she was reunited each night with her loved ones. More than any other piece of nineteenth-century mourning art, this well-known quilt vividly portrays the domestication of death that characterized nineteenth-century thought.

But not all bereaved women needed mourning images to draw comfort from the quilts binding them to their dead children. Begun in her teens, Margaret Conger's quilt top was appliquéd with vases of flowers and meandering vines, and it, too, became a bridge between the deceased Margaret and her surviving mother and sister.

Margaret Conger was born in 1831 in Shelbyville, Indiana, the third of George and Mary Conger's twelve children. Family records indicate that Margaret was crippled, and in fact she died when she was just twenty, having completed only the quilt top. Her mother carefully stored it for seven years. In 1858, when her youngest daughter, Emma, was twelve, Mary and Emma Conger finished Margaret's quilt. Emma was fifteen years younger than her sister and had been only five when Margaret died. Completing Margaret's quilt must have strengthened her bonds to a sister she hadn't known very long. The Conger family cherished the quilt for several generations, and in the 1930's it earned two ribbons in county fairs.

Mary and Emma Conger were not simply finishing a quilt. By completing Margaret's quilt they perpetuated their family ties and fulfilled a perceived obligation to Margaret. One aspect of the life-long duration of kinship bonds among nineteenth-century women was dependence. Experi-

Mourning quilt, by Elizabeth Mitchell, Lewis County, Kentucky, c. 1839, 81 × 85 inches, pieced and appliquéd cottons, with embroidery. A name or relationship written in ink on paper is sewn to each coffin. Collection of the Kentucky Historical Society, Frankfort, accession no. 59-13. Photograph courtesy of the Kentucky Historical Society.

ence had taught them that sooner or later they would need the help that could be provided only by their family's women. In many cases this would be the care of children left orphans at their mother's death; in this case the task left unfinished when Margaret died was her quilt.

Fourteen-year-old Laura Mahan had hardly begun her quilt when she died in 1848. She had been only three when her father, Artemas Mahan, had brought his family from Orangeville, New York, to Livingston County, Michigan, in 1836, the year when "land fever" reached epidemic proportions there.[25] Laura's mother had died when she was an infant, and her father had remarried, probably before the family left New York. With his new wife, Sarah, and his four children, Artemas Mahan was one of the first to settle the town of Marion, Michigan.

But seven years later, in 1843, Artemas died, leaving his widow and three children still at home. Sarah, unable to continue farming without her husband, took the children to Oberlin, Ohio, where their father's family lived.

It was a wise move. Artemas's brother, Asa Mahan, was president of the Oberlin Collegiate Institute, the educational branch of a utopian community established there ten years earlier. Its founders had created what they considered a model society based on traditional Christian values, and its members committed themselves to converting a sinful world and reforming it in Oberlin's image. The Oberlin Colony was structured as a family, with

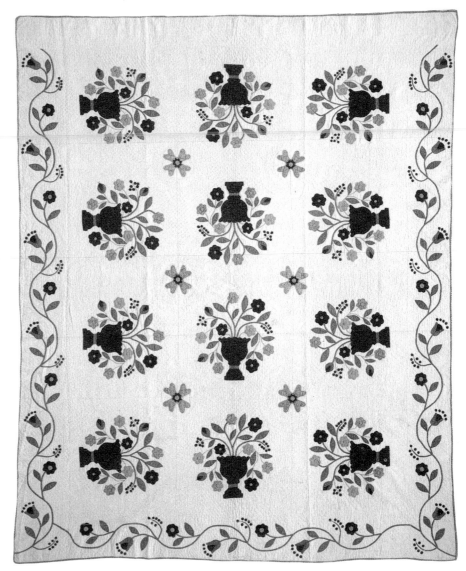

Basket *variation, begun by Margaret Conger, Shelbyville, Indiana, c. 1848, and completed by Mary and Emma Conger, Casey, Illinois, 1858, 77 1/2 × 97 1/2 inches, appliquéd cottons. Techniques include padding and embroidery. Collection of Ray Featherstone/The Country Shop, Westfield, Indiana.*

women at its moral center, and the evangelical values shared by its members contributed to a close-knit, strong community.[26]

Sarah and her stepdaughters Julia and Laura joined in the many religious, educational and reform activities of this new community, but young Samuel Mahan left after only a year. Julia married in 1846 and returned to Michigan. Sarah and Laura remained in Oberlin, and both attended school at the Institute. In

1848, while she was a student there, Laura died.

Sometime before her death, Laura had begun a friendship quilt. She had probably not progressed very far on it; only one inscription is directed to a child and most, dated after Laura's death, are messages of comfort to her grieving stepmother. And Sarah was indeed bereft. She had been Laura's mother since the child was at most three years old, and Laura was the last child at home. Like Margaret Conger's mother and sister, Sarah Mahan completed Laura's unfinished quilt, joining her in spite of her death in a familiar, domestic project which Sarah made still more personal by using scraps from Laura's dresses. In 1850 and 1851, she asked forty-four friends and relatives to autograph quilt blocks, then organized those blocks, like the community they represented, into a system of relationships. Laura's sisters, Hila and Julia, and their husbands adjoined each other in one row; Asa Mahan and his wife Mary were placed side by side, as were two engaged couples and a pair of student missionaries "destined for West Africa," as one wrote on the quilt. Other families were grouped in rows; and Sarah's block, establishing the quilt's purpose, shared the center vertical row with squares signed by her parents and her sister-in-law, Mary Mahan.

Sarah's family was truly fractured in 1850. Her maternal duties had ended with Laura's death two years earlier. Asa Mahan had resigned as president of the Institute and would leave Oberlin that summer with Mary and their children. Many of Sarah's student friends, some probably part of her household, were about to graduate. In 1851 she accepted the offer of a teaching position in a newly established school at Belle Prairie, Minnesota. Two blocks on her quilt indicate that their authors knew she was leaving.

Sarah had begun work on the quilt when her family was shattered by Laura's death. Now her family circle would again be broken, this time by Sarah's departure for Belle Prairie. The quilt that began as a link to one beloved daughter now joined Sarah to the family she would be leaving behind in Ohio.

But Sarah's maternal vocation did not end when she left Ohio. Some years later Elisabeth Ayer, director of the Belle Prairie school, described Sarah Mahan as "an experienced woman who knew well how to look after the 'odds and ends' in such a family, nurse the sick, and speak kind words to everybody, and make the children happy." [27] Sarah had become the mother of a new family.

Sarah Mahan, Mary and Emma

A c. 1884 photograph of a Shreve family reunion, Shreve, Ohio. Clara Carl Shreve is in the third row from the bottom, center, with her daughter (dressed in white) on her lap. This family homestead still stands and is being restored. Photograph courtesy of Roberta Thomas Thourot.

Conger, Elizabeth Mitchell and Margaret Weeden all made quilts joining their lives to past generations. But family did not end with the present. These women were well aware of their own eventual deaths. The eternal family that was so important to nineteenth-century women included granddaughters and great-granddaughters as well. And no thread running through the history of American quilts is stronger and more consistent than their use as links between women and their female descendants.

Sarah Mahan spelled it out in her bequest: "This quilt...I give & bequeath unto her sister... or...to her sister...otherwise to the oldest...granddaughter of their father...." Sarah was putting into words what so many quiltmakers felt: that the female family—past, present and future— was important, and that these generations were united by the quilts that were the work of their hands and hearts.

Rose of Sharon, *by Clara Carl Shreve, Shreve, Ohio, c. 1885, 77 × 78 ½ inches, appliquéd cottons. Collection of Roberta Thomas Thourot, a granddaughter of the maker.*

Clara Shreve's quilt still joins generations of women in her family. By the time her older daughter was seven, the quilt was almost all the family had that was Clara's. Clara Carl was born in Shreve, Ohio, in 1857. She was one of eleven children born to Georg and Christina Carl, German immigrants who had met and married in Ohio. When Clara was twenty-two she married Ezra Shreve, great-grandson of the town's founder, and within a few years had two children. Ezra's family was as large as Clara's; by the mid-1880's, family gatherings spanned five generations.

When Clara began her quilt her children were still very young.

She finished it just in time to move with her family to Mexico City, where Ezra had taken a job as a surveyor. Family history suggests that Clara may have been ill before she left Ohio; she is reported to have been easily fatigued as she worked on this quilt. Nevertheless she went to Mexico, and in April 1888 died there. Ezra was unable to care for his children, then only five and seven. Like Sarah Mahan in similar circumstances, he turned to family. More typically, he turned to his wife's family, and sent the children back to Shreve to be raised by Clara's

mother and sisters. Sadly, although he wrote to his daughters regularly, Ezra never saw them again.

Clara's quilt returned to Ohio with the children and since 1888 has linked Clara to her female descendants. The quilt passed first to Clara's daughter Maude, later to Maude's daughter Roberta. Eventually it will go to one of Roberta's two girls—the one who has a daughter of her own. Matrilineal descent, an important quiltmaking tradition for so many nineteenth-century women, is far from dead.

A c. 1895 photograph of Mary Edith Gorsuch and her children. From left to right: Mary Edith, Frances, Larkin, Virginia, John Edward, Robert and Eleanor. (This is the second Eleanor Gorsuch to own the quilt.) Photograph courtesy of Karen Hunter.

One of the most spectacular quilts to have survived the ravages of time and the Civil War is still in a family so well documented that its current members can recite from memory two hundred years of family history. This quilt was made in the second quarter of the nineteenth century for Eleanor Gorsuch, member of a prominent Methodist family that had settled Baltimore, Maryland, two hundred years earlier.

Ancestry was important to this family, and well into the twentieth century Gorsuch children were given family names. With little regard for genealogists of the future, Gorsuch parents in almost every generation called their sons John, Talbot and Larkin, and their daughters Eleanor and Elizabeth. Eleanor Gorsuch and her eight brothers and sisters were all named for family members, and this tradition reflected more than

a nominal bond. In every generation it engendered a warm, loving relationship as well.

Eleanor Gorsuch never married but was very close to her brothers and their children. She gave the quilt to her favorite nephew, John, while he was still a child. Many years later John and his wife, Mary Edith, bestowed on their oldest daughter both Eleanor's name and her quilt. Thus the quilt passed to a second Eleanor Gorsuch, and a family tradition was established. In time the quilt was given to this second Eleanor's beloved niece, also named Eleanor Gorsuch.

Because of the warm relationships within the Gorsuch family and the value they placed on their family's history, generational links between women with the same name were unusually strong. Except for its passage from the first Eleanor to her nephew, this quilt has descended not only through

women in the family but in each generation before the present one through women named Eleanor.

Eleanor's quilt was passed informally from women in one generation to women in the next. It was never left by will. The same is true of all the quilts discussed above for which there is an established provenance, and of most quilts which can be documented. It is even rare for a quiltmaker to inscribe a bequest on the body of her quilt, as Sarah Mahan did. If generational continuity was so important to nineteenth-century quiltmakers, why was the passage of quilts so informal, and Sarah Mahan's inscribed bequest so unusual?

The answer is probably found in laws dealing with property rights of married women. Before the mid-nineteenth century, wives in most states had no legal existence apart from their husbands. Any goods or money owned by a woman when she married, or inherited or earned during marriage, belonged to her husband. Even after her husband's death she could not reclaim it unless he left it to her by will. All she was entitled to, in some states, was the use during her lifetime of a third of her husband's real property (rights of dower).[28] Most quilts made before mid-century, therefore, were owned not by the quiltmakers but by their husbands.

In most cases, this would have presented a problem only when a husband died. If a deceased husband left a will, the family's quilts would have been dispersed as he directed. But if he died intestate,

Album, *probably made in Baltimore, Maryland, for Eleanor Gorsuch, Glencoe, Maryland, c. 1845, 103 ½ × 101 inches, appliquéd cottons. Techniques include padding, embroidery, fabric layering and ink work. Ink inscriptions include "For Ellenor A Gorsuch [emended from 'Gossuch']." Collection of Karen Hunter, a descendant of Eleanor Gorsuch.*

as Artemas Mahan did, they would have become part of his estate, to be distributed or sold at the discretion of the court. The only way a married woman could be certain that her daughter would receive a quilt intended for her, therefore, was by giving it to that daughter during her lifetime.

When the widowed Sarah Mahan made her quilt in 1851, she was head of household and no longer bound by such laws. Nevertheless, her experience when Artemas died eight years earlier had been tragic. After her husband's death, Sarah had been ill-advised by friends that Artemas's estate was under her control, and that there was no need to go through the courts to settle his debts. By law the farm would be inherited by his children, as would the money Sarah had brought to the marriage. In an attempt to keep the farm for the children, Sarah tried to settle Artemas's debts by giving her husband's creditors any items not needed by the family, and by selling the "crop on the ground." She even forfeited her rights of dower in an attempt to give "the dear ones committed to my charge, in consequence of the death of both their natural parents, such an education as will render them useful members of society."[29] Sarah's attempts failed; the farm and household goods were sold at auction; and Sarah turned to her husband's family for help.

Artemas died in 1843, and the next year the State of Michigan passed a Married Woman's Property Act which would have allowed Sarah to keep the money that had been hers at the time of her marriage. With that money exempted from her husband's estate, Sarah might have been able to purchase the farm for the family. With the estate in litigation until 1848, and with Hila and Julia still living in Michigan, Sarah could hardly have been unaware of the new law, or of the irony of her own legal situation.

Sarah's quilt was the one object holding her fractured family together: Sarah, in Ohio but about to embark on an unknown life in the distant Minnesota Territory; Artemas and Laura, both dead; her two remaining stepdaughters in Michigan; and their daughters, some not yet born. Sarah wasn't going to risk losing this icon. Her quilt represented her family and *was* her family. And family was too important to trust to the men whose laws so deprived their widows and orphans.

And so Sarah wrote her bequest directly on her quilt, where it could never be lost, set that block into the center of the top row, and entrusted it to the women in her family.

Sarah's faith was justified. Her quilt was preserved, and after 136 years has recently come home to the community in which it was made.[30]

REFERENCE LIST

1. Writers of prescriptive literature such as Lydia Sigourney, Catharine Beecher and Sarah Hale expounded frequently on this theme. A selection from *Godey's Lady's Book*, probably by Mrs. Hale, is characteristic: "Where, in this republican land, shall [woman's] field of work be fixed?... Not in the drudgery of life, the hard out-door employments, should her delicate hand be found. These are for man's strength of limb and physical energy to support bodily fatigue and exposure. Nor is woman's appropriate sphere in money-seeking pursuits." "[T]o amass wealth is not woman's province." "Home is woman's world; the training of the young her profession; the happiness of her household her riches; the improvement of morals her glory.... And all indoor pursuits she should be encouraged to learn and undertake, because these harmonize with her natural love of home and its duties, from which she should never, in idea, be divorced." "Editor's Table," *Godey's Lady's Book*, XLVII (July 1853), 84.

2. Nancy F. Cott, *The Bonds of Womanhood: "Woman's Sphere" in New England, 1780-1835* (New Haven: Yale University Press, 1977), p. 64.

3. John Mather Austin, "A Voice to the Married" (Utica: 1841), p. 38. Cited in Mary P. Ryan, *Cradle of the Middle Class: the Family in Oneida County, New York, 1790-1865* (Cambridge: Cambridge University Press, 1981), p. 147.

4. Ronald G. Walters, *The Antislavery Appeal* (Baltimore: The Johns Hopkins University Press, 1976), p. 94. Cited in Lori D. Ginzberg, "Women in an Evangelical Community: Oberlin 1835-1850," *Ohio History*, LXXXIX, 1 (Winter 1980), 86.

5. William Slade, *Fifth Annual Report of the General Agent of the Board of National Popular Education* (Cleveland: Steam Press of Harris, Fairbanks & Co., 1852), p. 9.

6. On female friendship in nineteenth-century America see Keith E. Melder, *Beginnings of Sisterhood: the American Woman's Rights Movement, 1800-1850* (New York: Schocken Books, 1977); Marilyn Ferris Motz, *True Sisterhood: Michigan Women and Their Kin 1820-1920* (Albany: State University of New York Press, 1983); and Carroll Smith-Rosenberg, "The Female World of Love and Ritual: Relations Between Women in Nineteenth-Century America," *Signs: Journal of Women in Culture and Society*, I, 1 (1975), 1-29.

7. "The Original Diary of Mrs. Laura (Downs) Clark, of Wakeman, Ohio," *Firelands Pioneer*, n.s. XXI (January 1920), 2312.

8. Helen Cowles to Mother, December 20, 1848. In *Grace Victorious; or, the Memoir of Helen M. Cowles* (Oberlin, Ohio: J. M. Fitch, 1856), p. 74.

9. Catharine Beecher, *The True Remedy for the Wrongs of Women* (1851), p. 116. Cited in Kathryn Kish Sklar, *Catharine Beecher: a Study in American Domesticity* (New Haven: Yale University Press, 1973), p. 198.

10. Linda Otto Lipsett, *Remember Me: Women & Their Friendship Quilts* (San Francisco: The Quilt Digest Press, 1985), pp. 61-83. For another Tolford family quilt, see pp. 47-57 of the same book.

11. Jessica F. Nicoll, *Quilted for Friends: Delaware Valley Signature Quilts, 1840-1855* (Winterthur, Del.: The Henry Francis Du Pont Winterthur Museum, 1986), p. 26.

12. Motz, p. 42.

13. Mary Tolford, Autograph Album, April 17, 1856, privately owned.

14. Mary Tolford, Diary, p. 27, privately owned.

15. Melder, p. 33.

16. Cott, p. 176.

17. Oberlin Maternal Association, manuscript minutes, October 6, 1852. Cited in Robert Samuel Fletcher, *A History of Oberlin College From its Foundation Through the Civil War* (Oberlin, Ohio: Oberlin College, 1943), II, 605.

18. Gertrude B. Jupp, "The Heritage of Milwaukee-Downer College: a Reaffirmation," *Milwaukee History*, IV, 2 (Summer 1981), 43.

19. Ellen K. Rothman, *Hands and Hearts: a History of Courtship in America* (New York: Basic Books, Inc., 1984), pp. 56-84. See also Cott, pp. 74-83; Motz, pp. 15-36; Smith-Rosenberg, p. 22.

20. E. H. Cawker to Pauline, October 13, 1888. Cited in Peter Merrill, "Pauline Adela Cawker" (unpublished paper), p. 3.

21. Merrill, p. 12.

22. Motz, p. 41. See also Linda Otto Lipsett, "A Piece of Ellen's Dress," in *Remember Me*.

23. Ann Douglas, *The Feminization of American Culture* (New York: Alfred A. Knopf, 1977), p. 209.

24. Stanley French, "The Cemetery as Cultural Institution: the Establishment of Mount Auburn and the 'Rural Cemetery' Movement," *American Quarterly*, XXVI (1974), 37-59.

25. For a witty and engaging account of life in Livingston County during the years the Mahans lived there, see Caroline Matilda Kirkland, *A New Home—Who'll Follow?* (1839; reprint ed. by William S. Osborne, New Haven: College and University Press, 1965).

26. Ginzberg, p. 83.

27. Elisabeth Ayer to Mr. Williams, July 28, 1891, Elizabeth [sic] Taylor Ayer Papers, Division of Archives and Manuscripts, Minnesota Historical Society Research Center.

28. Motz, pp. 23 and 121.

29. Sarah Mahan to Judge Kneeland, November 27, 1843, Livingston County, Michigan, Probate Court #280.

30. "Heirloom Quilt Returns to Oberlin After More Than 130 Years," *Quilter's Newsletter Magazine*, XVII, 3 (March 1986), 4-5.

RICKY CLARK is a quilt historian who has been widely published. She has served as curator for numerous quilt exhibitions and has lectured extensively. She is a founding member of the Ohio Quilt Research Project and an affiliate scholar at Oberlin College.

PIECES OF THE HEART

As quilting history in our era is being lived, it increasingly reflects a major development which enriches not only quiltmakers but creative women everywhere. Into the American experience, with strong roots and traditions underlying the national quilting revival, has come the gradual revelation that quilting no longer has particular national boundaries or a common heritage. It is flourishing in almost every part of the world, reflecting unique cultural experiences and revealing diverse personal identities.

The significance of the development of quiltmaking worldwide is not found simply in the images of a quilt shop in Singapore or a quilting co-operative in Soweto, however remarkable these occurrences might seem to those of us nourished by visions of pioneer quilters on the expanding American frontier. It is found in the astonishing fact that women who do not speak the same languages, who live on different continents and in different hemispheres and who do not share common cultural influences are simultaneously turning to quiltmaking as a medium of expression; in the process, they are establishing deep bonds throughout the world.

How is it possible that pieces of cloth should be the instruments for this profound connection? What can we learn from women in other lands who are strangers to us until we meet them through their quilts? Why is it that something crystallizes within us at that moment, a recognition that confers membership in what is now a worldwide sisterhood? It is in the relationships between the quilts and their makers, between the pieces of cloth and their lives, that possible explanations may be uncovered.

Quiltmakers who have not been exposed to American quiltmaking influences are working with both parallel and dissimilar habits and methodology. Most distinct from the American experience is the isolation in which many of these women work. While access to workshops and exhibitions is becoming more widespread, in many instances these women have little or no interaction with other practitioners. Consequently, they tend to develop an independent, self-reliant approach to their work which fosters freedom of expression.

Nowhere is this approach more evident than in the work of a former schoolteacher in the remote northern village of Schulp in West Germany. While this austere landscape is now home for Brigitte Fiss, it is her childhood during World War II that underlies her independent approach to quiltmaking. The solitude in which she finds creative freedom is an important part of that approach.

A slim, vivacious, middle-aged woman, Brigitte recalls that while more than half of her home city of Breslau was destroyed during the war, she was too young to share in the sense of loss. At the age of six, however, she demonstrated a strong, practical regard for survival. It began when her mother, hiding her fears about the approaching Russian army, gently told her daughter that they must leave their home. "We are going to move to the West, where we shall begin a new life." She then entrusted an important decision to her child. "You may choose one thing from your toys to bring with you. The rest

HANS-JOACHIM FISS

BRIGITTE FISS

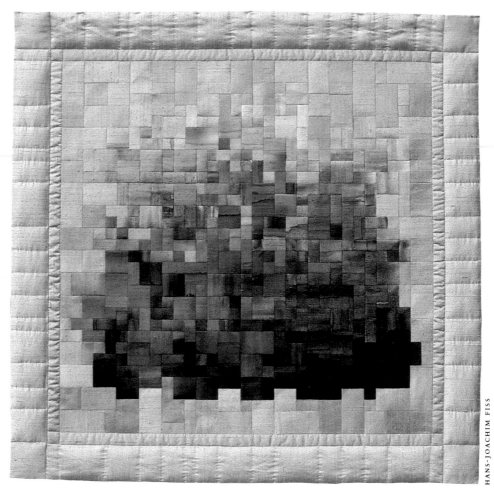

Winterdream of Summergarden, *by Brigitte Fiss, Schulp, West Germany, 1984, 33 x 33 inches, pieced in hand-painted silks and quilted with silk thread. Collection of the quiltmaker.*

must stay behind, because we can take only what we can carry. Find something you can take care of by yourself."

Brigitte hurried to her room to speak to her dolls. She held each one in turn as she inspected all her favorite playthings. Finally, she made her decision. As she, her mother, sister and grandmother left their lifelong home and possessions behind, the little girl carried with her to freedom in the West her small sewing bag. Inside was the treasure she had selected, a tiny pair of scissors.

The escape was successful and the four survivors began a new life in Hanover, where there was hardly a commodity that was not either scarce or unobtainable. The prudent child soon had many willing tutors, as women in their building discovered that she possessed a necessary tool for sewing and mending chores. During this period Brigitte established her lifelong habit of learning to do things for herself. Because there were no toys, she designed and made them from found materials. Every little thing assumed importance. Wool, for example, was collected from the knots in fence wires where sheep had brushed against them. "For Christmas that first year," she remembers, "I gave my grandmother a postcard with holes in it to pull the wool through. I also made a paper cone for saving the hair in the bathroom." She was seven years old.

Brigitte traces her creativity to the inventive use of materials at hand that she saw during the harsh postwar years. She recalls that creative ideas were always connected with the practical. "Being creative meant making the most of what you had and searching for new ways of doing things." She learned that "absence of things brings creativity," a lesson that would lead her to experiment widely in textile art.

MARY COYNE PENDERS

She taught herself to make felt and bobbin lace, to weave, to sculpt and to quilt. She used a cooking pot over a fire in her garden to make dyes from leaves, roots, bark, grass, flowers and onions. Enjoying her independence and wanting to find the colors she saw in nature, she began painting on white silk fabric, the hallmark of her present quilts.

She works in isolation, determined to be free, to find her own way. The resultant quilts have a dream-like beauty and a harmonious focus. Their softness and shimmer reflect Brigitte's love for natural beauty as well as her gentle temperament and delicate femininity. They are the antithesis of hardship and denial, economical in structure but profligate in the sensuousness of their texture. They display an absorption with color and detail. "I have in mind the ideas of color and shape, and I try to combine them, but always I am experimenting to the end to see what else I might do. It is planned, but I feel free to change at any time during the process," she explains.

Brigitte's quilts owe much to the instincts of the little girl who prized a pair of scissors as she was torn from her homeland. They are rooted in the practical and connected to the necessary. They are nourished by the experiences of growing up in a time and place where ingenuity was synonymous with creativity. Remembering the small scissors of her childhood and the women who prized them, Brigitte Fiss demonstrates to us that creativity can spring from adversity and that silken pieces of cloth can shimmer with renewed life.

Adversity of a different sort has played the central role in the development of one of the foremost quiltmaking artists in New Zealand. Jo Cornwall entered the art world when she left the psychiatric ward after a year and a half's stay following the birth of her youngest child. She is now a serene, unassuming woman of peaceful mien, but Jo's story is fraught with struggle, determination and perseverance.

It began on a fateful morning in the hospital when she awakened with a compelling urge to take responsibility for getting herself well. Her doctor opposed her decision to leave the hospital but, when faced with her determination, he gave her the key which she believes enabled her to overcome her illness. "Get a hobby," he advised, "and make it the

BARRY CORNWALL

JO CORNWALL

most important thing in your life."

Jo was forty years old when she enrolled in art school, where she produced abstract paintings as her mind slowly healed. When she made her first quilt, she knew at once that she wanted to exchange her paints for fabrics. For several years she developed her quiltmaking while serving as her husband's bookkeeper, managing to produce quilts in spite of the dirt, grease and noise of a machine repair shop. "Beauty can come out of chaos," she smiles. Now she works in a large room in her house in Te Puke, a small, isolated town of unspoiled beauty on the Bay of Plenty, surrounded by the design heritage of the native Maori people.

In her search for inspiration, Jo was attracted at once to this wealth of images close to the land which echoes shapes from the entire natural world to which the Maori are bound by myth and survival. The legends and values represented in their designs became a touchstone for her. The colors of the New Zealand landscape found their way into her quilts in vibrant hues and striking designs.

Jo thinks that in the beginning her quilts were too bold and graphic for people to consider for their beds or walls. It was hard for her to maintain her self-confidence when her work was not appreciated. She remembers the years of patient determination when she was not sure of the outcome. "Overcoming my mental illness has made me value every small achievement. It makes me even more grateful for my latent talents and it keeps me disciplined enough to work hard toward my goals," she says earnestly.

The quilts have a solidity to them that is connected to their traditional roots and to Jo's determination. Bold colors and large motifs echo her

Untitled, *by Jo Cornwall, Te Puke, New Zealand, 1980, 100 x 98½ inches, appliquéd cottons and cotton blends. The quilt was inspired by the kowhaiwhai, the designs painted on the rafters of the Maori meeting houses. Collection of Grant and Barbara Walter.*

surroundings and signify her hard-won confidence. Flowing, contoured quilting stitches suggest that she is expressing the serenity within herself on the surfaces of her quilts.

Jo's success is the result of the therapeutic value of the creative and repetitive tasks of the quilt-making process, applied to her quest for personal survival. She was thereby able to summon inner resources of courage and determination. In the struggles and the imagery of the native peoples of the "Land of the Long White Cloud" she found inspiration and stability. For Jo Cornwall, pieces of cloth are pieces of perseverance and healing.

The power of quiltmaking as a means of renewal is a recurrent theme in women's lives when they experience changes of circumstance and fortune. Gertrud Schupp, a silver-haired woman whose radiant looks and energetic manner belie her sixty-eight years, had a long and successful career in the textile industry, beginning with two years' study as a pupil of the Swiss color abstractionist Johannes Itten in 1937. Ten years ago, when the firm where she had worked for seventeen years declared bankruptcy, she was confronted with sudden financial uncertainty.

Gertrud confesses that at first she was scared. "How could a woman of fifty-eight face unemployment? What could I possibly do after all those years?" She knew that she needed to support herself, and she turned to what she knew best. "Always I was designing and loving and working with fabrics. Even though I have had to make money, there was deep within me the wish to do something creative." Her eyes are mischievous when she declares that "I was not scared for very long. I decided like lightning to quilt!"

She began immediately, with time and fabrics in ample supply; when she had spent a year making

Persian Court, *by Gertrud Schupp, Munich, West Germany, 1980, 62 x 80 inches, pieced, appliquéd and quilted by machine in velvets, brocades, silks and wools. Techniques include padding and layered embroidery. Collection of Wulf Schupp.*

GERTRUD SCHUPP

quilts, her photographer son provided her with a professional portfolio. Publication in an important magazine brought orders for twenty quilts, and her new life as a professional quiltmaker began. "For me," Gertrud confides, "this shows how something good can come from something bad in your life. My security was won back by making good with what I knew and what I had."

Her quilts conjure rich images, often filled with experiences from other times and places. The surfaces are elaborate with padded appliqué shapes; they are sumptuous and sculptured, as though, after years of highly disciplined employment, finally she was free to be as profligate as she liked. Gertrud's

MARJORIE COLEMAN

free use of fabric and color is made possible by her skill in utilizing her extensive fabric collection.

Gertrud Schupp's quilts often detail the architectural features of Art Nouveau and the ornamental opulence of the sixteenth-century Persian court, two of her favorite periods. Her historical and fanciful images contrast vividly with her modest Munich apartment where she draws and designs on a small dining table and sews at a machine in a tiny kitchen. The limitations of her physical space are no impediment to her rich imagination or to the joy with which she greets her work. "It is like a fever," she exults. "I spent twenty years telling others what to do. Now I can work alone and I can learn inside myself."

In spite of themes from art history, years of studies at textile school and the major influence of Itten on her color work, Gertrud Schupp does not live in the past. Her outlook and her manner are contemporary. She states firmly that "I am always in the future, because I was told once that you have not to look back or you are growing old." Her forward-looking vitality has contributed to a future that is filled with commissions, exhibitions and promotions for her recent book.

Gertrud Schupp has more pieces of cloth than most of us. Deciding to use them to make quilts "like lightning" was an auspicious decision for a quiltmaker whose quilts have the luster of a life devoted to textiles and the spirit of a woman who welcomes the future.

The concept of time, both present and future, is prevalent in the outlook of many quilters outside the American experience. Whether by artistic choice or temperament, these women have a strong bent toward originality as the foundation of their quilts. Marjorie Coleman speaks about this attitude when she tells us that "I am an Australian of this day and age, and I want the images, effects and colors that I use to arise out of my own experience rather than to speak of another time and place."

Living outside the isolated city of Perth, Western Australia, Marjorie is a university wife who has raised five children. She is free to pursue quiltmaking and feels strongly about the immediacy of her creative ideas. A slight woman, appearing almost smaller than she really is, Marjorie is intense, nervous, enthusiastic and mercurial. She likes to sketch from life for her themes. Plants, animals and natural shapes are her preoccupation. "My images and symbols are mine," she maintains. "I try to be polite to old quilts, but they do not fire me in the way contemporary ones can."

Marjorie prefers to intrigue rather than to excite. In order to reflect her own experience and background instead of repeating shapes from a different time, she looked to the spectacular wildflowers of the Australian bush for design possibilities. In flowers with evocative names like the kangaroo paw, the purple bell, the macrocarpa and the grevillea she found an elaborate living world of fantastic form and color. The quilts which reflect her vision of this small cosmos are a series called *Dullflowers,* the title a wry salute to those who find only boredom in the bush landscape.

The Australian bush is the ideal companion to Marjorie's shy and withdrawn temperament. Her complex nature responds to the intricacies of the natural world with recognition and delight. Using needle and thread to illustrate in exquisite, meticulous detail the images from her own time and place, she demonstrates that she is indeed an Australian of this day and age.

It is important that her quilts record this unique heritage and that they have received widespread recognition in Australia; but the significance of Marjorie Coleman's work for her sister quilters around the world is that she was able to see the possibilities in ordinary and even ridiculed forms, and then to make them spectacular with pieces of cloth.

Dullflower #3: Banksia, by Marjorie Coleman, Cottesloe, Western Australia, 1984,
63 x 71 inches, pieced and appliquéd cottons, cotton blends and rayons, with
embroidery. Collection of the quiltmaker.

The gift of seeing possibilities is an integral part of all creative endeavor, but it is the unique personal identity of the quiltmaker as well as the influence of her cultural experiences which give us fresh insights. In the university city of Cambridge, England, an attractive, middle-aged woman is caught up in the possibilities inherent in the quilting process itself. Deirdre Amsden is straightforward, cheerful and untidy; a charming, attractive woman, she works in a studio converted from a former chapel, sharing space with her artist husband.

In speaking about possibilities and her approach to quiltmaking, Deirdre says, "My ultimate goal is to make the patchwork and the quilting interdependent, so that each needs the other to become a coherent whole." Experiments through a wide variety of styles and techniques led her to the creation of her *Colourwash* quilts, a developmental series working with Liberty lawn prints. "I noticed their blending qualities," she explains, "and I had an inspiration. Could I turn things around? I was using contrast in my patchwork in order to define the shapes. What if I used the blended prints to dissolve the shapes?" Deirdre liked the possibility of using the fabrics in the way that a painter would portray colors and light. Once the idea of not defining the shapes took root, she discovered that quilting had a more important role to play and could be used to blend the patchwork even more.

"I wanted to create areas of contrast within the washes of color," she says, "and this in turn led to realizing that I could make it appear as though the washes of color were transparent or laid on top of one another. I wasn't able to do this with water colors in art school, but I discovered I could do it with fabric." The pieces in this study reflect Deirdre's self-containment—they are very small squares, and she patiently works on their arrangement with the concentration of a jigsaw-puzzle addict.

The subtle pointillist imagery of these disciplined designs shows the emergence of her goal, the wedding of the square patchwork shapes to the curvilinear quilting stitches. Echoing her own personality traits of confidence and caution, Deirdre observes that "quiltmaking is full of contrasts. It's so easy to learn, but I find it endlessly complex to master." She enjoys the contrast of the challenge of design with the repetitive tranquillity of execution.

Deirdre's quilts are widely exhibited and published, and she is the founder of the English Quilters' Guild. She has taught twice in South Africa for

DEIRDRE AMSDEN

the Zamani Soweto Sisters Council, where she found inspiration in the contrast between the harshness of their lives and the beauty of their fabric art. She also finds striking contrasts between the absolute simplicity and the fantastic detail of the work of the

Colourwash Overlay II, by Deirdre Amsden, Cambridge, England, 1986, 25½ x 25½ inches, machine-pieced cottons. Hand-quilted with silk thread. Collection of the quiltmaker.

ANDI ZAI

ADELHEID GUBSEK

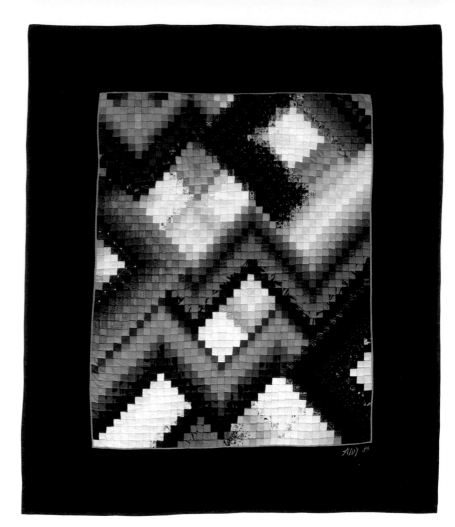

Kleinka 2, by Adelheid Gubsek, Basel, Switzerland, 1985, 46½ x 55 inches, pieced and quilted in cottons and cotton blends. Signed and dated in embroidery. Collection of the quiltmaker.

Spanish architect Antonio Gaudí. The ability to recognize contrasts and to make them work for her in fiber art has enabled Deirdre Amsden to remind us of the unlimited possibilities of pieces of cloth.

Contrast is sometimes very dramatic between the lifestyle and the creative expression of the quiltmaker. It is one of the great underlying strengths of quilting that it can fulfill so many different needs for the diverse worldwide community of quilters. Among those whose life is in direct contrast to her fabric art is a twenty-seven-year-old quiltmaker in the Rhenish city of Basel, Switzerland. Adelheid Gubsek is an independent, moody young woman who likes to daydream. Her sister Ruth sees her as capricious and self-willed, while her boyfriend Felix finds her charming and reserved. She likes eccentric clothes that help her look like an artist.

Her friends, who call her Aidy, think that her quilts express her immediate outlook on life and experience. Before she found what she was searching for, Aidy had an unhappy adolescence. "This is because my biggest wish, ever since I have been able to think, has been to express my ideas, my feelings, my impressions. I did not know how I was going to do this, but I knew I had to find a way."

The search led her through three years of education as a teacher of handcrafts, which brought happiness because "every day was an adventure, with new things to learn and old things to get to know better." But when the time came for practical courses in theory and methods, Aidy was faced with drastic change. "The truth is," she confesses, "that I did not like to educate children who were not interested in the subject." Troubled about the reality of the situation, she retreated into daydreams about leading a different kind of life. She dreamed about escaping from reality, floating with her boyfriend on a magic carpet toward the rainbow. "In the technique of patchwork I saw the possibility to express my dream, and my first quilt, *Rainbow Flight,* was born."

Employed as a teacher following her schooling, Aidy was unhappy with the school regulations limiting her creativity and with the students' unwillingness to work to her standards. "My real work was to give orders: do this and don't do that," she recalls sadly. An identity crisis was followed by severe depression when her "rainbow flight" came to a hard end: "My lover left me to live in Berlin, and I was in a state of total confusion. But life goes on, doesn't it?" she sighs. "Again I turned to patchwork and found the help I needed. It was the very best therapy for black thoughts." Aidy made a new quilt but still felt she had missed her vocation.

At this time she made a major decision that changed the direction of her life. She decided to save money until she could take one year off to create quilts as a full-time occupation. "But I couldn't wait so long! Life is funny sometimes," she says wistfully. "I found a new boyfriend. This time he did not leave me for Berlin, but for Paris. And so my next therapy quilt was born."

Finally Aidy was able to take her sabbatical. Describing this precious time, she says, "I felt in my heart a big silence, a gladness. I was lonely the whole day through, out of society, but I became used to my new life and I loved it. I did not want to do any other kind of work." Unfortunately she soon found that, while she could sell most of her quilts, she did not have enough money to continue. Reluctantly she obtained another job and quilting time was again severely limited.

Not satisfied with this solution, she decided to rearrange her life so that she could have blocks of time necessary for creative work. She found a factory job where she was able to work for two months and then take two to three months off to make quilts before returning to the factory to make more money for daily living. Aidy describes this divided life: "At the same time that the inspirations for my quilts were going through my head, I had to arrive at new understandings with many different people and learn a whole new way of life. It is the only way for me to live my life as a quilter. I've been able to make twenty big quilts, but it is only the beginning. The more I do, the more I see new possibilities, new combinations of colors and forms."

Aidy's quilts are a direct contrast to her life of personal and financial uncertainty. Her images are precise and controlled; her quilts are models of order and stability. Instead of therapy, she now finds patchwork a means of expressing her thoughts and impressions about the world. She uses the diamond shape repeatedly because she says that "in the diamond technique I see each diamond as a feeling; then it changes to a person. If I cannot unite human beings in reality, I can do it on my quilts. These are the feelings my quilts keep in my heart."

Her willingness to work at a factory job which provides the freedom to pursue her true vocation is a poignant indication of the depth of Aidy's commitment to quiltmaking. From the chaos of her life she has taken pieces of cloth and fashioned them into a coherent reality. She shows us that stamina and determination can overcome obstacles to creativity, and what may be impossible in real life can be attained on the structured surface of a quilt.

The stories of these six women of different nationalities, languages and cultures illuminate the human connection that makes quiltmaking a unique and powerful medium of expression throughout the world. In their lives we recognize the everyday trials of hardship, illness, insecurity, unhappiness and ordinary existence; we see also the ultimate victories of courage, determination, ingenuity, acceptance and joy. The physical boundaries that separate us from these creative women are overcome by the common experiences and aspirations that bind us. In no way is this more dramatically expressed than in the unifying strength of quiltmaking—the medium of shelter and tranquillity. For women everywhere, pieces of cloth are pieces of the human heart.

MARY COYNE PENDERS, a quilting teacher who lives in Vienna, Virginia, has been working with students in the Washington, D.C., international community since 1975. She is known throughout the United States for her conference workshops and lectures. Travel teaching in Australia, Canada, Holland, West Germany and New Zealand has led to extensive research in contemporary quiltmaking abroad. Author of *Quilts in the Classroom—A Guide to Successful Teaching,* she specializes in professional development seminars for women. She is currently at work on a book-length version of this material.

SHOWCASE

COMPILED BY RODERICK KIRACOFE

◀*Friendship,* made by members of a church group in Falmouth, Maine, 1857, for Joseph Colesworthy, 99 × 98 inches, pieced and appliquéd cottons. Ink inscriptions of dates and names include "Mother," "Grandmother" and "Henry." Collection of Margaret C. Hudson, a grand-niece of Joseph Colesworthy. Submitted by The Vermont Quilt Festival, Northfield, Vermont.

Chasing Red Dogs, by Linda MacDonald, Willits, California, 1985, 92 × 92 inches, machine-pieced and hand-appliquéd cottons. Quilted by hand. Collection of Kathleen and Robert Kirkpatrick.

Log Cabin—Light and Dark, by Ursula Egger-Graf, Volketswil, Switzerland, 1980, 55 ½ × 55 ½ inches, machine-pieced and hand-quilted cottons. The "working" apron of the quiltmaker's grandmother is included in this remembrance quilt which is dedicated to her. Collection of the quiltmaker.

Crewel work spread, c. 1840–1860, origin unknown, 84×88 inches, embroidered wool yarn on pieced wools, cut for a poster bed. Collection of the Shelburne Museum, Shelburne, Vermont. Submitted by The Vermont Quilt Festival, Northfield, Vermont.

KEN BURRIS

Crazy variation, c. 1880–1900, found in Massachusetts, 55 × 65 inches, pieced and appliquéd silks, satins and velvets, with embroidery. "Betsey Richards" is stamped within a stamped cartouche on the back of this quilt. Collection of Gail van der Hoof and Jonathan Holstein.

Receding Bars/Orange-Green, by Ardyth
Davis, Leesburg, Virginia, 1985, 59 ½ ×
63 ½ inches, pieced, painted and quilted
silks. Tied with cotton threads. Collection of the quiltmaker.

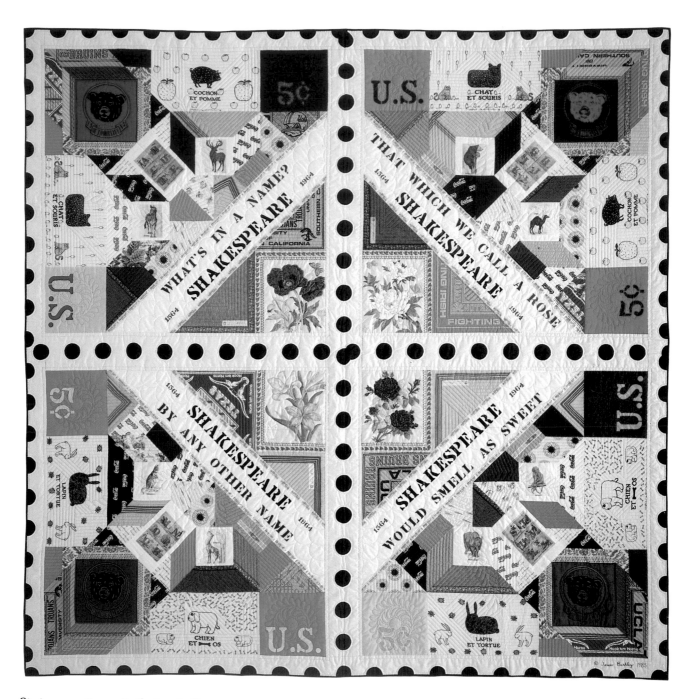

Shakespeare Stamp Quilt, © 1985 Teresa Barkley, Astoria, New York, 102 × 102 inches, machine-pieced and hand-appliquéd cottons and cotton blends, painted by hand, with printed scarves, linen tea towels and pages from two antique linen children's books. Quilted by hand. Signed and dated in embroidery. Collection of the quiltmaker.

Eagle, c. 1870–1890, Indiana, 84 ½ × 82 inches, pieced and appliquéd cottons, with embroidery. "Mary A. Zellers, Winamac, Ind." is stamped in ink. Collection of Sandra Mitchell, Columbus, Ohio.

The Memory, by Gerlinde Anderson,
Riverside, California, 1986, 65 × 76
inches, machine-pieced and hand-appliquéd cottons, silks, corduroy and chif-
fon, some of which have been over-dyed
and painted, cut as if for a poster bed.
Hand-quilted with cotton and metallic
threads. Collection of the quiltmaker.

Palampore, by Hannah Reed, York, Maine, 1820, 111 × 104 inches, pieced cottons, cut for a poster bed. "Hannah Reed 1820" is embroidered on the back of this quilt. Collection of Linda Hilliard. Submitted by The Vermont Quilt Festival, Northfield, Vermont.

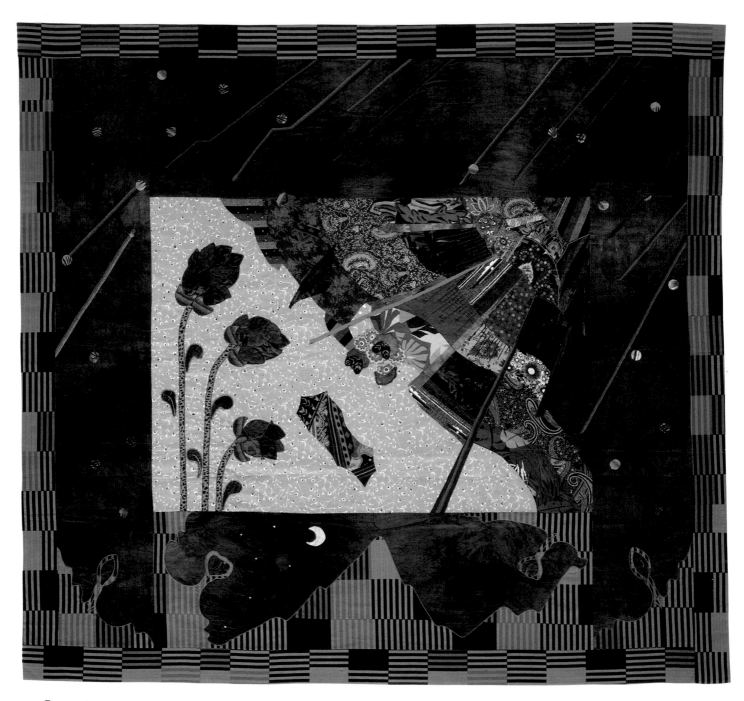

Cosmos, by Kumiko Sudo, San Jose, California, 1984, 69 ½ × 65 inches, pieced, appliquéd and embroidered cottons. Quilted by Chizuko Watanabe, Tokyo, Japan. Collection of Kumiko Sudo.

Center Square, c. 1900–1920, from the
Levi Lapp family, Lancaster County
(Pennsylvania) Amish, 82 × 82 inches,
pieced wools. Collection of Bryce and
Donna Hamilton.

Unknown pattern, by Susan Robb, c. 1860-1870, Arkansas, 77 × 81 inches, pieced and appliquéd cottons. Techniques include reverse appliqué and embroidery. The quilt depicts a Confederate view of the Civil War. In the center, troops of both the North and the South are represented. A pelican is toppling an eagle in a symbolic defeat of the North. According to Robb family history, the yellow calico dog represents the family dog which followed the quiltmaker's son off to war. Collection of The Museum, Texas Tech University, Lubbock.

42

Charlie Kreiner Quilt, by Christina Ramberg, Chicago, Illinois, 1985, 64 × 84 inches, machine-pieced and hand-quilted cottons. Private collection.

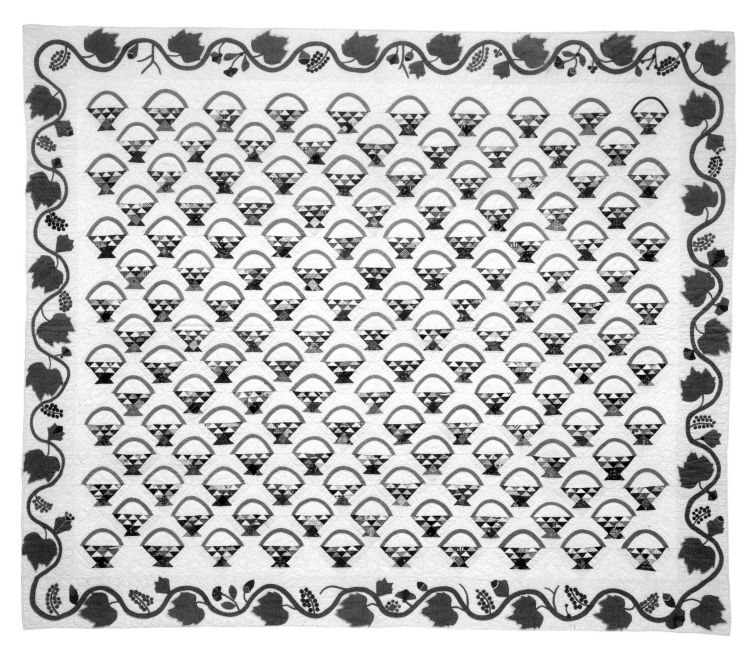

Basket, by Minnie Wheeler, near Cook-
ville, Tennessee, c. 1910–1930, 91 × 77
inches, pieced and appliquéd cottons.
Techniques include embroidery and padding. The majority of the printed fabrics
date from between 1880 and 1910. Collection of Andrea Hays. Photograph
courtesy of Patricia Smith, Washington,
D.C.

A Camouflaged Affair, by Steve Strata-
kos, LaGrange, Illinois, 1984, 69 × 55
inches, appliquéd and quilted by machine
in polyesters, satins and cottons, some
hand-dyed. Signed in paint. Collection
of the quiltmaker.

The Sea of Japan in Winter, by Shizuko Kuroha, Tokyo, Japan, 1983, 78 × 78 inches, pieced cottons. Some of the fabrics are fifty years old and made from *kasuri* (men's kimonos). Collection of the quiltmaker.

Album, made by Amanda C. Collinsgru, Montgomery (now Silver Spring), Maryland, c. 1880–1900, 63 ½ × 62 inches, appliquéd and pieced silks, satins and velvets. Techniques include embroidery and padding. Collection of Grace Parker, granddaughter of the maker. Photograph courtesy of Alice M. Simensen.

49

WHEN THE SMOKE CLEARED

BY DOROTHY COZART

*H*ome decoration was paramount in the lives of late-Victorian women, and that fact was due in large part to the decorative-art movement that coincided with the 1876 Centennial Exposition in Philadelphia.[1] Magazines and books on decoration directed women to embellish their homes so as to improve the lives of their families. Readers were told that the embellishment could be accomplished by any woman, no matter what her financial situation, and to do so, women were encouraged to use what today would be termed "throw-away items." Items such as left-over beads, lace, braids and ribbons could be used to create household articles that would make "artistic statements" in the makers' homes.[2] The results of all this beautification of household articles became known as "fancywork."

As quilt historians such as Penny Mc-Morris have already revealed, it was considered imperative that every moment be filled with useful activities, and that fancywork could cure any idle woman's boredom or nervousness.[3] In her *Crazy Quilts*, McMorris quotes *Dorcas Magazine* (October, 1884), which calls fancywork "the best and only rest possible to many a nervous woman. Remember, monsieur, she has not the resource of a cigar."[4] Although women may not have had the "resource" of smoking cigars, they did have the

"resources" of the ribbons that usually accompanied the cigars, and later they had the silks that were inserted in cigarette packages and the flannels that were included in or with other tobacco products.

Very little has been written about fabrics that were used in the merchandising of tobacco, which include cigar ribbons, cigarette silks and cigar flannels. Even less has been written about the quilts that were made from them. When placed in the context of the time from which they came, roughly the years 1870 to 1920, both the fabrics and the quilts become very interesting. Not only do they reflect the importance of home decoration during that time, they also suggest the impact of tobacco usage on late-Victorian and early twentieth-century society.

*T*he technique for using cigar ribbons in quilts and other household articles was well known by women doing fancywork. It was the same as that used in the construction of *Log Cabin* quilts: strips of cloth were applied to a background fabric. However, the addition of surface embroidery, usually feather stitching, was, it appears, deemed necessary: embellishment was universally popular. And in that way cigar-ribbon quilts are closely related

From upper left, in clockwise order: Orange printed cigar ribbon (collection of the author); blue printed cigar ribbon (collection of Kenneth Silverman); butterfly cigarette silk (Silverman); Hamilton King's "Redondo Beach Girl" cigarette silk (Silverman); Turkish Trophies gift slip for Hamilton King silks or other premiums (Silverman); front and back sides of Fatima coupon for cigarette silks (author); woven cigarette silk (author); Players Tobacco card showing how their flag silks could be utilized (Silverman); J. Wix hand-woven Mediterranean silk in its descriptive folder (Silverman); American flag cigar flannel (author); plush Oriental carpet with fringe in its presentation envelope (collection of Delmas Ford); and Indian rug cigar flannel (author).

Facing page: Detail of a cigar-ribbon pillow sham, c. 1870–1910, origin unknown, embroidered silks. Shown are woven ("Electric" and "Harvard") and printed silks. Collection of the author.

to crazy quilts, which were being made at about the same time and were extensively decorated with embroidery.

Many women must have recognized that it would be fashionable to make something useful of the brightly colored ribbons that were used to tie groups of cigars together and to wrap around cigars sold in boxes. These ribbons were plentiful by 1870, and by 1880 cigar smoking had become America's favorite form of tobacco use. Consequently, thousands of small cigar factories had sprung up all over the United States. All cigars were wrapped by hand and could be produced using few tools other than hands.[5] Narrow bands of cloth, and later ribbons, had always been used to tie bundles of cigars together so that factory workers, who were paid by the bundle, could receive their proper wages. From

this practice grew the custom of using ribbons with brand names on them when the cigars sold. The bundles, when sold, might consist of as few as seven or nine cigars or as many as fifty or one hundred.[6] Federal revenue laws required every cigar leaving the factory to be boxed, since boxes were easier to count and tax.[7] But the bundles were also tied with ribbon, and different colors of ribbon were used to designate the various grades of cigars (this page). Both the boxes and the ribbons served as billboards, designed to catch the eye of the consumer. About 1900, some manufacturers began using paper bands on each cigar, since more advertising could be placed on them. Eventually ribbons with brand names on them were discontinued in favor of the bands.[8]

The brand names were stamped at

Cigar-ribbon quilt, c. 1870–1910, origin unknown, 65 × 76 inches including border treatment, embroidered silks. Collection of the United States Tobacco Company (Museum of Tobacco Art and History), Nashville, Tennessee.

regular intervals on the ribbons, and women took advantage of this fact by arranging the names to create patterns on the surfaces of their quilts (this page). Some quilts contain many different brand names, and there were thousands of them.[9] However, entire blocks, or even whole quilts, might be made up of ribbons bearing one or a few popular names, such as "Blackstone," "Quincy" or "Londres." The colors of the ribbons were used creatively. Although most ribbons were orange (sometimes referred to as gold) and yellow, they were also produced in blue, red and white. Some quilts were constructed so that a contrasting color became an integral part of their design (this page).

Elaborate woven ribbons were also used by some manufacturers. Brand names such as "Electric" and "Harvard" were woven into the fabric, and borders, curlicues and other decorative effects were added (page 50). It is hard to believe that cigar ribbons such as these would not have been used in crazy quilts. However, since positive identification can come only if brand names are visible, the ribbons

are almost impossible to identify. Perhaps most women shared the feelings of Heloise Herbert, the heroine of a story which appeared in *Godey's* in 1884. "The Career of a Crazy Quilt" relates the difficulties encountered by two friends in obtaining suitable fabric scraps for their respective crazy quilts. The story consists of a series of letters, and in one letter Heloise complains:

Ned is such an absurd brother! This morning he came in with a lot of those nasty little yellow cigar ribbons all in a tangle, and offered them to me for my crazy quilt. But I don't intend to mind ridicule or difficulties.[10]

Heloise solves the problem by marrying a salesman for The American Silk Mills, and he furnishes the friends with all the silk necessary to complete their projects.

No doubt makers of cigar-ribbon quilts would have sympathized with Heloise and her friend and their collection woes. The number of smoked cigars necessary to generate enough ribbons to make a quilt is staggering. Some women solved this problem by making smaller articles like throws, which were used in parlors, or small pillow covers, larger pillow shams or table covers.[11] If, however, a woman wanted to make a full-size bedcover, she could use the same method Heloise and her friend used and collect fabric from relatives and friends. A woman might be fortunate enough to have a relative who operated a cigar store,[12] or her husband might collect them for her in the same way a man who was a traveling salesman in the Pacific Northwest is known to have done.[13] Although there is no documented proof that any women married a man to benefit from his cigar ribbons, it is certainly reasonable to imagine that a quilt made from the ribbons could have helped persuade a young man to marry her. *The Art Amateur*, one of the decorative-art publications, reported: "One of the ambitions of a young man of fashion nowadays is the possession of a crazy quilt, made up of patches contributed by the ladies of his acquaintance."[14] Would not a quilt made from the ribbons from his own cigars have been equally welcome?

While the quilts that were made of cigar ribbons may not be considered beautiful today, they successfully echo the taste of the era from which they came.

Probably the major tobacco companies were aware that cigar ribbons were being used in quilts, and almost certainly most companies had noted the popularity of crazy quilts. So it is not surprising that about 1900[15] two more fabric items, cigarette silks and cigar flannels, were introduced and used in selling tobacco products. Whether they were created because they could be used in quilts and other household items cannot be proved. What probably is true is that cigarette silks, then called "silkies," were introduced at a time when tobacco companies were very interested in getting women to smoke.[16] Cigar flannels, which were used concurrently with silks as inserts in packaging, may have been considered more masculine. Not only were they made of cotton flannel, a rougher fabric, but also they were packaged with cigars and other tobacco products, such as cut plug, which might have been considered more suitable for men than women (page 51). The attractive silks were usually made of satin and bore varied and colorful lithographed designs. Certainly they resembled the patches that women had been making or buying for use in their crazy quilts for years (page 51). Even many of the motifs were the same: flags, butterflies, flowers, animals and birds. There were also silkies of beautiful women and famous people. These, like the photographs printed on cloth that were just becoming easily accessible, were included in quilts. Perhaps most appealing of all to quiltmakers was that the silkies were free. Each silkie was one of a series, and the number of available series is mind-boggling. The American flag could be obtained in several sizes, along with state flags, flags of other nations and flags with rulers of other nations pictured in the foreground. In addition, there were domestic animals, wild animals, breeds of dogs, fowl, birds, butterflies and moths. There were also portraits of Indians, U.S. presidents, baseball players and famous actresses. Especially there were beautiful girls—bathing girls, girls with flags of all nations, girls in fancy dress, girls and more girls. One series was even designated "feminine types." Flannels were produced in fewer series, the most common one being flags (this page). The more unusual flannels are the Indian-blanket and Oriental-rug series, some of which have a fringe at each end of the flannel, and which were sometimes made of plush as well as flannel (page 51). All of the fabric items were attractively designed, and illustrators and photographers vied for the opportunity to create material that would be used in them. The artist Hamilton King became so well known for his beautiful girls that the series he created is known by his name among collectors (page 51).

Cigar-flannel quilt, c. 1900–1920, origin unknown, 90 × 92 inches, cotton flannels, with cotton gauze bunting material as a flounce. More than likely, the large American flag flannel at the center of this quilt was a special premium offer (see text, page 55). Collection of Kenneth Silverman.

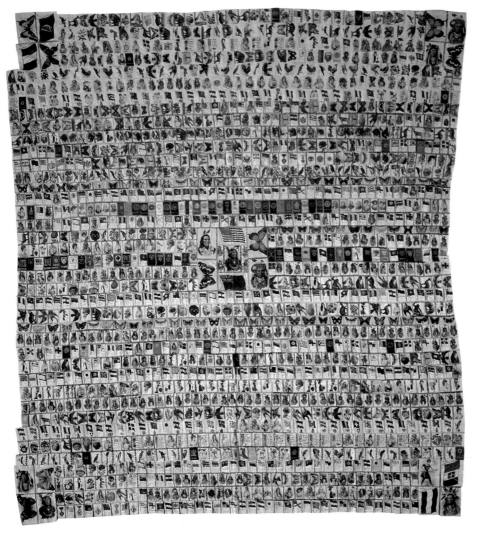

Cigarette-silk quilt top, c. 1900–1920, origin unknown, 84 × 98 inches, embroidered silks. This top contains printed and woven silks depicting, for example, U.S. presidents, bathing girls, wild animals, domestic animals, Indians, cities, months, seasons of the year, fraternal orders, beautiful women, flowers, fruits, butterflies, sayings and children. Collection of Kenneth Silverman.

The insert cards came in series, as did the ones printed on cloth, so it was easy for the manufacturers to convert to cloth when they deemed the time was right. Collecting complete series of advertising cards had already become a favorite hobby by the time silkies and flannels were introduced. Although single silks or flannels are sometimes found in crazy quilts today, it is easier to find quilts, or quilt or pillow tops, made entirely of them. Rarely is there creativity demonstrated in quilt designs using silks and flannels. They are most often simply applied to a background cloth in rows, one small rectangle after the other (this page). Simple feather stitching or even cross-stitch is the embroidery pattern used, in marked contrast to the elaborate embroidery used in most crazy quilts. It seems reasonable that the cigarette-silk and cigar-flannel quilts were made in order to preserve collections of various series (this page, pages 53, 55).

Changes were taking place in early twentieth-century society, and these changes are reflected in the simplified designs of these quilts. For one thing, the decorative-art movement was dying if not dead even before silks and flannels were inserted into tobacco packages. By 1900 many of the decorative-art magazines had ceased publication, and women's magazines had turned their attention to "scientific efficiency."[17] A clean, uncluttered home was deemed necessary in decors inspired by the new American Arts and Crafts movement. The overabundance of elaborately decorated items was passé.[18] Women were beginning to find interests outside the home, and they did not have either the time or the inclination to spend long hours cleaning a cluttered house and doing fancywork. This is not to say that crazy quilts, for example, were not being made, but their designs and embroidery were greatly simplified.[19]

Some tobacco companies surely realized that a

By the time it became economically advantageous for the tobacco companies to start printing their advertising material on cloth, it was a simple matter to do so. Cards with advertising on one side and attractive pictures on the other had been used with tobacco products for about twenty years. The Duke Tobacco Company, which was to become the powerful American Tobacco Company, began, in about 1885, using a small picture card as a stiffener in their paper-wrapped cigarette packages. As a result, sales skyrocketed, and every cigarette maker began making similar cards, which were called "inserts." Technically, an insert was not given away; it was sold with a product and available only in that way.

new generation of women—doing less fancywork than their predecessors—needed help in designing household items using silkies, and that they also needed to be reminded of the many items that could be made with them. Player Tobacco inserted a card of instructions along with the silkie in each cigarette package, such as:

The satin inserts may be stitched (herring-bone style) on a piece of silk, satin or other material. As indicated, some *simple* [italics mine] embroidery adds greatly to the attractiveness of the finished article. Other things which can be made of the satin flower inserts are screens, bed spreads, lamp shades, sewing bags, hatbands, portieres, pin cushions, doilies, table centers, masquerade dresses, belts, bands for the hair, kimonos, pillow tops, ties, piano drapes, table cloths, doll's dresses, teapot cosies, egg cosies, mantel drapes, comforters, handkerchief bags, sideboard covers, dresser covers, covers for chairs, parasols, etc., etc.

A colored sheet showing some of the uses to which these inserts could be put will be mailed post free on receipt of your name and full postal address [page 51].[20]

*T*he tobacco companies were aware that women had less time for creating decorative household items and began offering premiums. Premiums were merchandise that could be ordered with coupons[21] inserted in tobacco packages. An example is the pillow top described in a Fatima coupon as "flower decorated, white satin, 24 inches square." The pillow has individual silks placed attractively around a central picture of a bouquet of roses. Printed cross-stitch around each silk creates the illusion that the silks are hand-stitched. The pillow top could be obtained by sending sixty coupons from any Liggett & Myers (makers of Fatima) tobacco products. Items made of cloth were the most frequent premiums offered. Larger silks and flannels than those used as inserts (such as 7 × 9 inch Hamilton King girl silkies) could be obtained with Turkish Trophies gift slips.

The Player Tobacco Company has been mentioned, and it is important to note that it is a British, not American, concern. The use of tobacco inserts was international, although most foreign inserts were of paper rather than cloth. Flannel inserts were apparently issued only in the United States, but silks became popular in South America as well as in Canada, England and

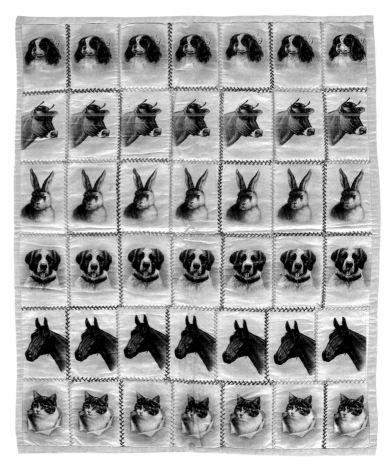

Cigarette-silk comforter, c. 1900–1920, origin unknown, 29 1/2 × 35 inches, tied and embroidered silks. Collection of Kenneth Silverman.

other countries of the United Kingdom.[22] Godfrey Phillips, a British company, produced fifty different series of silks, and this company awarded prizes for the best handmade articles utilizing them. They are known to have given prizes for "cushion covers, counterpanes, and even garments."[23] J. Wix, another British company, produced a particularly beautiful set of hand-woven silks. Woven in the Mediterranean area, each silk of the series was enclosed in a folder which contained a description of the flower pictured on the enclosed insert (page 51).[24] Inserts continued to be used abroad long after they had been discontinued in the United States.

There is no agreement in the scant resources available as to why American tobacco companies decided to stop filling their packages with sundry inserts and coupons. Tobacco usage had become big business by 1900, and the use of inserts did have an important effect on tobacco marketing at that time. One conglomerate, the American Tobacco Company, had virtually succeeded in monopolizing

55

the tobacco industry, largely through its advertising efforts. It is commonly believed that the inserts and premiums produced by this company cost far more than the tobacco itself. In 1911 the American Tobacco Company was declared a monopoly by the government, and it was eventually broken up into four smaller companies through the use of the anti-trust laws. These companies and the cigarettes they became best known for are: American (Lucky Strike), Liggett & Myers (Chesterfield), Reynolds (Camel) and Lorillard (Old Gold). Although the smaller companies continued to use inserts and premiums, by 1917 all four had stopped.[25] No doubt the production of the costly items was a financial burden to the smaller companies. Also, by the beginning of World War I, millions of Americans, both men and women, were smoking cigarettes. The tobacco companies must have believed that the insert and premium advertising campaigns, although successful, were no longer required, and after the war mass-media advertising replaced them.

Although neither cigar-ribbon quilts nor those

Cigar- and cigarette-silk comforter, c. 1900–1920, origin unknown, 88 × 86 1/2 inches, tied and embroidered silks, with silk flounce. ▶ *Collection of the author.*

made with cigarette silks and cigar flannels are extremely rare today, they are found seldom enough to be considered curiosities. It goes without saying that many of them were probably worn out or discarded, but more than likely only a relative few were ever made. After all, cigarette silks and cigar flannels were issued after fancywork had lost much of its popularity. In the case of the cigar-ribbon quilts, it is quite possible that many of them were made prior to the height of the crazy-quilt fad, and many women may have chosen to spend their time making the far more popular crazy quilts. Besides, many religious groups were opposed to tobacco in any form, and women in particular decried the influence of the "noxious weed."[26] It is entirely believable that women who felt this way, even though their husbands smoked cigars or cigarettes or chewed tobacco, would never have used fabric associated in any way with "that filthy habit" in quilts. And, while it is true that many women started smoking cigarettes between 1900 and 1920, many other women would never have used items designed to "tempt women to sin," no matter how beautiful those little patches and ribbons might have been.

Many thousands of the tobacco-related fabrics still exist. A few collectors have extensive collections. More than likely, many lie unused in attics and basements. However, the extant quilts made from cigar ribbons, cigarette silks and cigar flannels prove that some were used resourcefully by quiltmakers who were striving to remain as calm as the cigar-smoking men in their lives.

Cigarette-silk and cigar-flannel quilt, c. 1900–1920, origin unknown, 88 1/2 × 70 inches, pieced silks and cotton flannels. Collection of Kenneth Silverman.

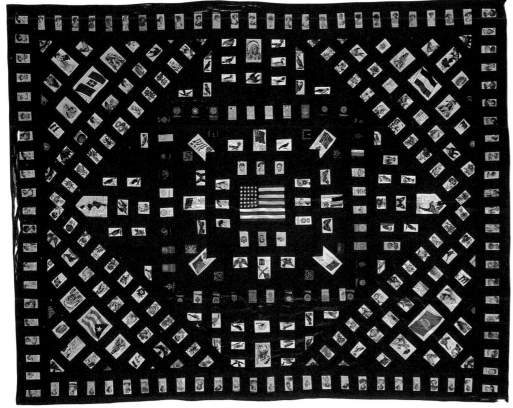

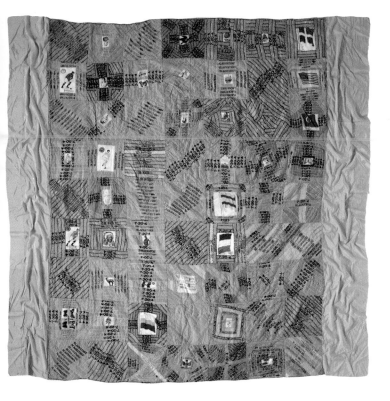

Reference List

1. For a good discussion of the decorative-arts movement, see Virginia Gunn, "Crazy Quilts and Outline Quilts: Popular Responses to the Decorative Art/Art Needlework Movement, 1876–1893," *Uncoverings 1984,* ed. by Sally Garoutte (Mill Valley, Calif.: American Quilt Study Group, 1985), pp. 131–152.

2. See the photographs of a Victorian home in Penny McMorris, "Victorian Style: Vintage Photographs of an American Home," *The Quilt Digest 2,* pp. 26–33.

3. Penny McMorris, *Crazy Quilts* (New York: E. P. Dutton, Inc., 1984), pp. 13–15.

4. *Dorcas Magazine,* October 1884, p. 263, quoted in McMorris, *Crazy Quilts,* p. 15.

5. Robert Heimann, *Tobacco and Americans* (New York: Mc-Graw-Hill, 1960), p. 94.

6. John B. Kline, "A Tool Collectors' Guide to Tobacco Farming and Cigar Making Tools" (unpublished paper, 1975), p. 39.

7. Tony Hyman, *Handbook of American Cigar Boxes* (Elmira, N.Y.: Arnot Art Museum, n.d.), p. 3.

8. Many quilt enthusiasts confuse ribbons and bands, calling ribbon quilts "cigar-band quilts." Ribbons are cloth; bands are paper.

9. J. R. Burdick, ed., *The American Card Catalogs* (New York: Nostalgia Press, 1967), p. 41.

10. Dulcie Weir, "The Career of a Crazy Quilt," *Godey's Lady's Book,* CIX (July 1884), 78.

11. A table cover made like a flag is shown in Thomas K. Woodard and Blanche Greenstein, *Crib Quilts and Other Small Wonders* (New York: E. P. Dutton, 1981), p. 83.

12. As related in Diana McLachlan, *A Common Thread... Quilts in the Yakima Valley* (Yakima, Wash.: Yakima Valley Museum & Historical Association, 1985), p. 50.

13. Joyce Gross, *A Patch in Time* (Mill Valley, Calif.: Mill Valley Quilt Authority, 1973), p. 26.

14. " 'Crazy' Quilts," *The Art Amateur,* October 1882, p. 108.

15. There is little agreement on when silk and flannel inserts first were used. The author chose to use the earliest date found.

16. Burdick, p. 83. This has also been mentioned by other collectors in conversations with me.

17. Gunn, p. 147.

18. For a further discussion of the effects of the Arts and Crafts movement, especially in regard to quiltmaking, see Penny Mc-Morris and Michael Kile, *The Art Quilt* (San Francisco: The Quilt Digest Press, 1986).

19. McMorris, *Crazy Quilts,* p. 26. Cigarette silks and cigar flannels are found incorporated into crazy quilts. If the quilts are undated, the presence of these fabrics would help in dating, unless the tobacco items have been added later to replace other deteriorating fabrics. A quilt seen by the author had been extensively repaired, under direction by the owner, with several silks from the U. S. presidents series.

20. Notice that there is no use of the word *quilts* in this exhaustive list; bedspreads and comforters are mentioned, however. The insert was from Montreal, Canada.

21. Coupons were also called "gift slips" and "gift certificates."

22. Frank Doggett, *Cigarette Cards and Novelties* (London: Michael Joseph Ltd., 1981), p. 9.

23. Doggett, p. 44.

24. *The Guide to Cigarette Card Collecting,* 12th rev. ed. (London: Albert's of Kensington, 1986), p. 15.

25. Christopher Benjamin and Dennis W. Eckes, *The Sport Americana Price Guide to the Non-Sports Cards* (Laurel, Md.: Den's Collectors Den, and Lakewood, Ohio. Edgewater Book Company, Inc., 1981), p. 5.

26. The author grew up in a Midwestern Methodist home, and the terms used here for tobacco and smoking are the ones the women in her family and community used during the 1930's and 1940's.

The author would like to thank the following people for their help: Harry L. Branchard, a member of the International Seal, Label and Cigar Band Society, Kenneth Silverman and Delmas Ford, collectors of tobacco silks and flannels, Jacqueline M. Key, Curator and Manager of the U. S. Tobacco Museums in Greenwich, Connecticut, and Nashville, Tennessee, and David R. Wright, Manager of the Museum of Tobacco Art and History, Nashville, Tennessee.

DOROTHY COZART, a native Oklahoman and grandmother of four, taught in high school and at Phillips University in Enid. She serves on the board of directors of the American Quilt Study Group, and she has published three articles in their annual journal, *Uncoverings.*

Until recently, it was not known whether quiltmaking was an integral part of women's needlecraft in early Australia. As a British colony, started in 1788, Australia was born between the final years of the American War of Independence and the outbreak of the French Revolution.

New South Wales (NSW) was founded as a penal colony, after the cessation of transportation to America in 1783. It offered little scope for decorative arts, amongst its tents and houses of wattle and daub, and the women who were transported for life hardly had time for needlecraft and fancywork, except for the most essential and primitive. But, as the colony developed, there were also women who were wives of government officials, emancipists, immigrant free settlers and, by the 1830's when the community had evolved into a wealthy pastoral society, these women of the colony had the time and means for patchwork.

But the history of Australia also mirrors that of the United States of America, where families pushed westward in bullock wagons in search of agricultural land, to live in isolation in an unknown environment. Did the wife or daughter of a small settler who had been born or married in the bush of NSW in the mid-nineteenth century have the time or necessity for quiltmaking?

Throughout the nineteenth century, the development of the colony mainly reflected

Annette Gero

the social and technological changes in England and Europe. The gold rush in the mid-nineteenth century brought an amalgamation of different cultures into the society and, by the late nineteenth century, an Australian-American cultural exchange was fostered by the establishment of trade routes. Australian patchwork in the nineteenth century appears to have been influenced by all these conditions, and it is within the context of these changes that the nature of Australian women's lives and the patchwork needlecraft which they created comes to life.

Patchwork in Australia appears to be as old as the colony itself. It was the women of Newgate Prison in England, sentenced to transportation to NSW for life, who were taught to make patchwork quilts by the Quaker prison reformer Elizabeth Fry. From 1817 to 1843, Elizabeth Fry supervised the women who were to make the appallingly crowded and long voyage to Australia and supplied them with an occupation for the voyage—patchwork—which would produce items which could be sold on arrival. The sum thus raised meant that the convicted women would not be completely destitute after disembarkation.

With the support of the British Society of Ladies and wealthy Quaker merchants, each convict woman was provided with one Bible, two aprons, one small bag of tape, one ounce of pins, one hundred needles, nine balls of sewing cotton, twenty-four hanks of colored thread, one small bodkin, one thimble, one pair of scissors and two pounds of patchwork pieces.[1]

Elizabeth Fry's concern for the welfare of the female convicts on their voyage is reflected by a letter she wrote on April 20, 1818, to the first chaplain of the colony, Reverend Marsden, enquiring whether the occupation of patchwork had produced beneficial results:

[I] have taken great pains with the females of this ship...given them [patch]work to perform...and have laid off the little money belonging to each in those things that are likely to sell at Port Jackson [Sydney]. I much fear however that all these useful [occupations] will be laid aside as soon as the ship proceeds to sea and I should feel much obliged if you would give me an account of the effect they produce, for if good results from it, some important changes may take place in regard to the future ships sent out.[2]

The scheme was obviously successful: Elizabeth Fry organized the women on a total of 106 ships, and many of the 12,355 female convicts transported to NSW came under her care.[3] Women could be transported for a crime as small as "Quakers denying any oath to be lawful, or assembling themselves together under the pretence of joining in religious worship" or "persons found guilty of steal-

Quilts and Their Makers

ing cloth from the rack."[4] These women and prostitutes were transported together with convicted murderers. Thus, employment on the voyage was regarded as important occupational therapy.

A report in 1838 to the Select Committee on Transportation in the British Parliament on the conduct of the female convicts during the voyage states:

They have some occupation during the voyage: they are allowed certain patch-work which keeps them in some degree occupied. . . . As far as I have been able to collect from surgeons who have attended convict vessels and from those persons who have attended female convicts on their arrival, the giving them this employment has had the effect of occupying their minds . . . but it does not last to the end, they get over their work by the time they have gone two thirds of the voyage.[5]

This perhaps explains why some of the patchwork quilts produced on the voyage were sometimes disposed of on the way. In 1818 one of the ships, *Maria,* called at Rio de Janeiro where some quilts were sold for a guinea (one pound and one shilling) each. Otherwise the quilts were sold in Sydney on arrival.

For some reason there was a ready market for patchwork quilts in New South Wales. It has been surmised that

perhaps to those far-off exiles in so strange and different a world, where the stars themselves are foreign, a patchwork quilt looked more homelike than anything else they could imagine, and underneath its folds, thrown across their

Elizabeth Fry and the Convict Women, *engraving by Jerry Barrett, published by William Lucas and Co., London, England, May 1, 1863. Collection of David Ell.*

in 19th-Century Australia

grass hammock or their bed of fern... they could dream themselves back into the english cottage bedroom of their childhood.[6]

As far as we know, the patchwork quilts which were made by the women on these voyages have not survived in Australia. Perhaps one will be discovered, but that is unlikely, as they were utilitarian pieces which carried with them the taint of the convict and were probably disposed of as soon as possible.

However, two quilts of convict origin, and associated with the work of Elizabeth Fry, have been bequeathed to Strangers Hall Museum, Norwich, England. The first quilt contains hexagons appliquéd onto a cream linen background (this page). The second quilt is pieced together from

Central Medallion, by women prisoners under the guidance of Elizabeth Fry, probably England, early nineteenth century, 87 × 102 inches, appliquéd cottons on linen. Collection of Strangers Hall Museum, Norwich, England. Photograph courtesy of the museum.

eighteenth-century silk on linen and contains early nineteenth-century English and Indian printed fabrics with embroidery. The central embroidered squares are surrounded by printed strips and borders. "Elizabeth Fry, Elizabeth Baker and John Fry 1817" is embroidered in fine red cross-stitch in the center.

Perhaps the earliest surviving quilt made in Australia is that attributed to Elizabeth Macarthur (page 61). Not all the women arriving in Australia in that early developing period were of convict origin. Anne McMahon, in her study of "The Lady in Early Colonial Society,"[7] defines three types of women who arrived before 1850—the "female," the "woman" and the "lady." These groups were defined not by birth but by their status on arrival.

The "females" were usually convicts or the wives of convicts. Those that were not assigned to settlers as servants (who became the property of their masters during the term of sentence) were assigned to the Female Factory in Parramatta (a house of correction) and employed as laundresses and seamstresses. Although the women were employed picking, spinning and carding wool, there is no record of any patchwork having been produced.[8]

The second group, the "women," were free settlers, wives or single women trying to better themselves in a new life. These people were encouraged to immigrate by Commissioner Bigge's report of 1822, which stressed the need to build up a free section of the population in the Australian colonies.[9] These women were

probably too busy and too poor to allow themselves needlework except for absolute necessities.

A "lady" needed the qualification of birth and a superior rank by virtue of her husband's position in the colony. She must have arrived free. She had no dealings with the convict class except in the role of mistress, and women of this class were called "fair," "gentle," "cultivated" and "intelligent." These women were not without occupations, however. They ran the household (with three or four servants), the dairy and, in their husbands' absence, the property also.[10] Nevertheless, it is the needlework of these ladies which now survives. By the 1830's, handsome stone buildings were the homes of the rich, adorned with silver, china, furniture and fabrics from England and the Continent. Within these environments the household occupations of the lady of the colony included needlework of the type which was fashionable in England at the time. Some of these pieces have been treasured and handed down to subsequent generations, such as Elizabeth Macarthur's quilt (page 61).

Elizabeth Macarthur, her army officer husband John and their baby Edward sailed to Australia with the Second Fleet on January 17, 1790, together with their servants. Elizabeth, just twenty-three years old, kept a journal of their voyage. They sailed on the *Neptune* together with five hundred convicts who were starved, brutally treated and seldom allowed access to the sun. During the voyage, 123 of them died. Elizabeth and her family had half of a partitioned cabin, which was in immediate contact with those of the convict women. Her boy and her servant were taken very ill and

Left: Hexagon, attributed to Elizabeth Macarthur, c. 1835–1840, 144 × 144 inches, pieced cottons and cotton chintzes. The quilt is shown on a Macarthur bed. The bed hangings are made from a reproduction of 1832–1845 "Emily" chintz. Collection of the National Trust of Australia (NSW). Courtesy of Elizabeth Farm, Parramatta.
Right: Portrait of Elizabeth Macarthur, at age seventy-nine, by William Nicholas, 1845. Private collection.

her daughter, born prematurely on the voyage, did not survive.[11]

They arrived at NSW five months later, on June 28, 1790, after what has been described as one of the most disastrous voyages in the history of transportation to Australia. However, Elizabeth, as the first free lady in the colony, drew strength from her English upbringing in the household of a country parson, John Kingdom, and her letters reflect a keen interest in the colony. Her husband was to become one of the most famous men in the colony, and his breeding of merino sheep and export of wool to England were the beginnings of Australia's wool industry. John Macarthur is featured on the current Australian two-dollar note.

Elizabeth Macarthur's quilt was made in the late 1830's. By this

time she had had nine children (five boys, three of whom survived, and four girls, of whom three had survived) and lived at Elizabeth Farm (named after her) in Parramatta. Her boys had been sent to England for their education and returned to the colony in 1817 to work in the family business, and her husband had made several trips back and forth, on one occasion leaving her to manage the property for eight years. He had died in Sydney in 1834.

Elizabeth Farm was her first real home, and it remained so for all of her life. It was a grand house by colonial standards and contained four rooms, a large hall, a cellar and adjoining kitchen and servants' quarters. Elizabeth was in her sixties when her quilt was given to her third daughter, Mary Isabella Bowman, who married

James Bowman, Esq., the Principal Surgeon of the Colony in 1823. Cambrics, chintzes, muslins and dimities were all imported by the Macarthurs from England and in 1826 Elizabeth Farm was refurnished. The quilt was possibly made from the left-over fabric.[12] Elizabeth Macarthur died at Elizabeth Farm in 1850 at the age of eighty-three.

Early families like Elizabeth Macarthur's and those "free" immigrants who sailed to Australia before the 1860's needed to bring with them everything that was required for the voyage as well as all their household goods required for settlement in Australia, even their bedding, including patchwork quilts. One of the earliest examples of such a quilt in Australia is a chintz quilt[13] (this page) made in England between 1810 and 1825 by Marianna Lloyd (1796–1880). Marianna married William S. Button in 1826 and her sister Harriet married William's brother Thomas Button. Together they emigrated to Launceston, Van Diemen's Land (Tasmania) in 1833 aboard the ship *Forth,* and with them they brought their entire belongings, including the chintz quilt. The Button family was extremely wealthy, and in 1853 William Button became the Lord Mayor of Launceston.

Many of the quilts made before 1860 which have turned up in present-day Australia without any provenance are possibly, like the Lloyd quilt, of English origin. The patterns found in quilts of this period, regardless of their origins, reflect English influence, mainly hexagons and central medallion quilts similar to the early quilts produced in Colonial America.[14]

Besides Elizabeth Macarthur's quilt, we know from diaries of early Australian "ladies" that quilting or patchwork was regarded as a highly desirable pastime. Annabella Boswell, who lived with her uncle Major Archibald Clunes Innes (who owned many sheep and cattle stations in the northern district of NSW), wrote in her diary of 1844:

Marion was busy finishing a patchwork table cover of silks, the pieces cut in diamond shape of three different shades. These, when sewn together, form rows like boxes. The effect is very good. She kindly gave me the patterns and we at once looked out all our pieces of silk and began to make one for our aunt.[15]

Annabella certainly lived in the upper class of the colony. In 1847 the family received a visit from Lady Mary Fitzroy, the Governor's wife. Their home was described as "as commodious and well appointed as any English country house."[16]

It is not known whether Annabella's quilt still exists, but it is probable that the pattern was copied from an English quilt which was brought to the colony. The *Tumbling Blocks* pattern is one which is best put together using the English paper template technique of oversewing. This technique was very much the pre-

serve of the "genteel ladies" of the late eighteenth and early nineteenth centuries, and it was they who set the fashions of the time to be copied later by colonial women.[17]

It is an interesting conjecture that the block arrangement of diamonds was in use in Australia before it reached the United States. Barbara Brackman, in "A Chronological Index to Pieced Quilt Patterns, 1775–1825,"[18] states that "the hexagon mosaic was represented as was simple diamond patch work, but the Baby's Blocks arrangement of diamonds was not found in the era

Central Medallion, by Marianna Lloyd, England, 1810–1825, 90 × 104 inches, pieced in a variety of chintzes, including some which are printed by block or roller. Collection of Audrey Meredith, great-granddaughter of the quiltmaker.

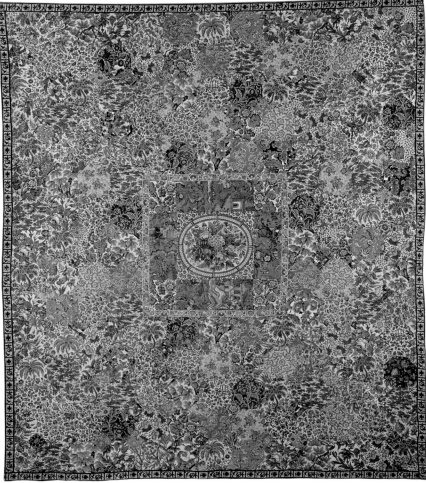

studied." She suggests that the earliest example of this pattern found to date in the United States is 1854, ten years later than Annabella Boswell describes this pattern in Australia.

Hexagon *with* Tumbling Blocks *border, table cover, c. 1860–1870, Tasmania, 61 × 63 inches, pieced velvets and silks, with fringe. Collection of the Queen Victoria Museum and Art Gallery, Launceston, Tasmania.*

In 1851, gold was discovered in both New South Wales and Victoria by two miners returning from California, E. H. Hargreaves and J. Hiscock. Excitement ran high. The Victorian towns of Melbourne and Geelong were almost emptied of men, cottages were deserted, businesses were left without staff and ships were deserted in Port Phillip Bay. The small towns near the diggings, Ballarat and Sandhurst (Bendigo) overflowed with people. Housing was tents, lean-tos, bark huts or a few yards of hessian stretched between two trees.

By the end of 1851, the news of the discoveries had spread around the world. In England, Scotland and Ireland, gold seekers scrambled for passage on ships bound to Australia, and Americans, who believed the Californian gold-rush days of 1849 had vanished, took ship for NSW or Victoria. The gold rush was responsible for the single largest immigration to Australia. Prior to 1851, Australia was treated with derision by the British newspapers, depicted solely as a country of convicts. However, after the discovery of gold it became a place where one went to seek a fortune and to better one's way of life. During the potato famine in Ireland in the 1840's, many of the poorer population migrated to America, as the fare to America was five times cheaper than that to Australia. But during the 1850's, after the discovery of gold,

many middle-class Irish families chose to emigrate to the Australian colonies. One such family was the parents of Jeanette Dick.

Mary and John Dick, a seamstress and a clerk, emigrated from Belfast, Ireland, to the gold fields of Sandhurst (Bendigo) in 1854. With them they brought their two young children, Hugh (born 1845) and Jeanette (1847). Life in the gold field was rough to begin with, housing consisting of no more than a tent, which was sometimes given rough outer walls of split slabs of eucalyptus and a mud chimney. Women were scarce in the gold field at this time, most having been left in the cities, although women and chil-

dren were known to sift the shoal and tailings for the men.

By 1854, when the Dicks arrived at the diggings, tradesmen had set up businesses in the goldfield towns and erected large wooden buildings. The first schools were established in Catholic churches, and miners began to build log-cabin huts. Hotels, boarding houses and saloons were built, and some of the land was developed for agricultural produce. Horse-drawn coaches ran daily to Melbourne to deliver the gold, and hundreds of tons of goods per day were carted back into the mining towns. The streets became lined with businesses offering blue and red serge shirts,

MARK BARKTEOVITCH

Californian hats and other mining commodities.

Bendigo became a vigorous and diversified community. By 1855, balls and theater were advertised and tailors and women's outfitters established themselves to cater to the women who had appetites for silk and satins in the fanciest of gear. According to a newspaper of the time, "Young misses began to appear in brand new bonnets, carrying a parasol of the finest quality silk and sedate matrons came out on the streets in gaudy silk dresses." Those men who had struck it rich appeared in "swooping tailcoats of silks and brocades."[19]

Jeanette Dick's father made enough money in 1854 to purchase a small general store, used as a drapery, in the main street. As the business grew, Jeanette worked as a saleswoman in the shop, so from the age of fourteen (girls went to school only until they were thirteen) she grew up amidst bolts of silks and satins and expensive brocades. The Australian side of the family were much luckier than the Irish family they left behind. When Jeanette's uncle died in Ireland in 1862, she was bequeathed "whatever meal and potatoes she may require" together with "the beds, bedding and table linen belonging to the house."[20] Whether Jeanette inherited a patchwork quilt from her uncle is not known, but in 1864 she started to collect fabrics to make her own *Log Cabin* quilt (page 65) in silks and velvets which were in vogue at that time.[21]

In 1868, at the age of twenty-one, Jeanette married Irish-born Thomas Thomas, who owned a draper's shop in Emerald Hill, South Melbourne. As part of his business as a haberdasher, Thomas

A c. 1904 photograph of the Dick family, from left to right: quiltmaker Jeanette Thomas (née Dick), her granddaughter Adele Grant, her daughter Ethel Eva Florina Grant and her mother Mary Jane Dick.
Courtesy of Margaret Anne Thomas, granddaughter of Jeanette Dick.

Thomas traveled by horse-drawn buggy to the gold-mining towns to sell his stock of fabrics, hooks and eyes, and needles and had become acquainted with Jeanette on many of his trips. Jeanette assembled her quilt in 1867 as part of her trousseau. The couple moved to South Melbourne and set up Thomas' Drapery in Clarendon Street, which is still standing today.

In 1879, at the age of thirty-five, Thomas died, leaving Jeanette with five children under ten and pregnant with a sixth child. There was no option for Jeanette except to take over the draper's business in order to support her own children. She worked very hard and supported her family well. The *Log Cabin* must have been very special to her, as when she died she left her precious patchwork to the male child she was carrying when Thomas died. The quilt

is now in the possession of his daughter, also a seamstress.

By the 1870's, the gold hysteria had slackened. However, many people stayed in the gold-field towns, as the soil was excellent for agriculture and stock. In 1862, railways from Melbourne to the Ballarat and Bendigo gold fields had been completed and farmers could get their produce to Melbourne within a day.

Many old Australian quilts originated in this area during this period. Although the quilts of the first half of the nineteenth century were mainly hexagon, *Tumbling Blocks* or central medallion quilts, an indigenous style of patchwork developed during the latter part of the nineteenth century.

Such a quilt is that of Mary Ann Bruton, which was started

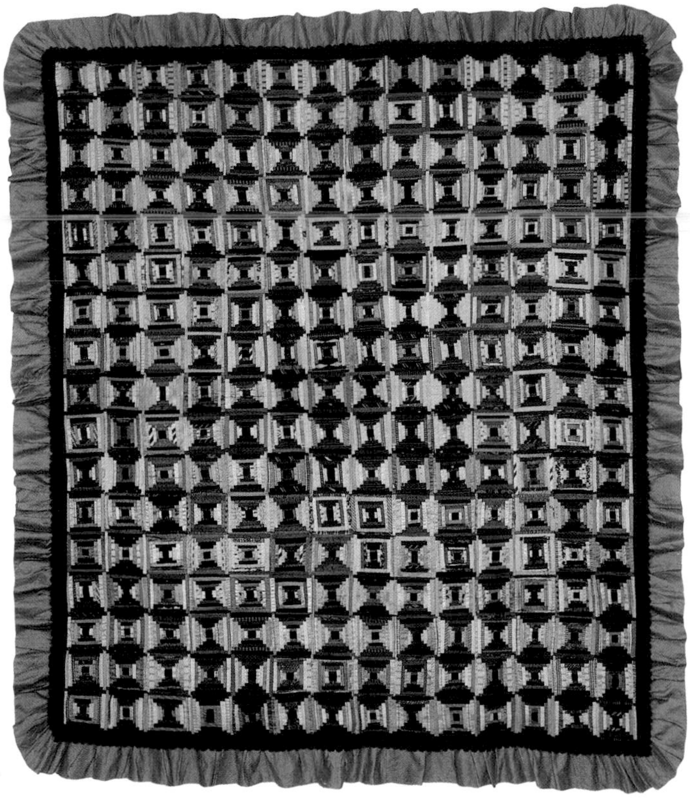

JAN TUDOR

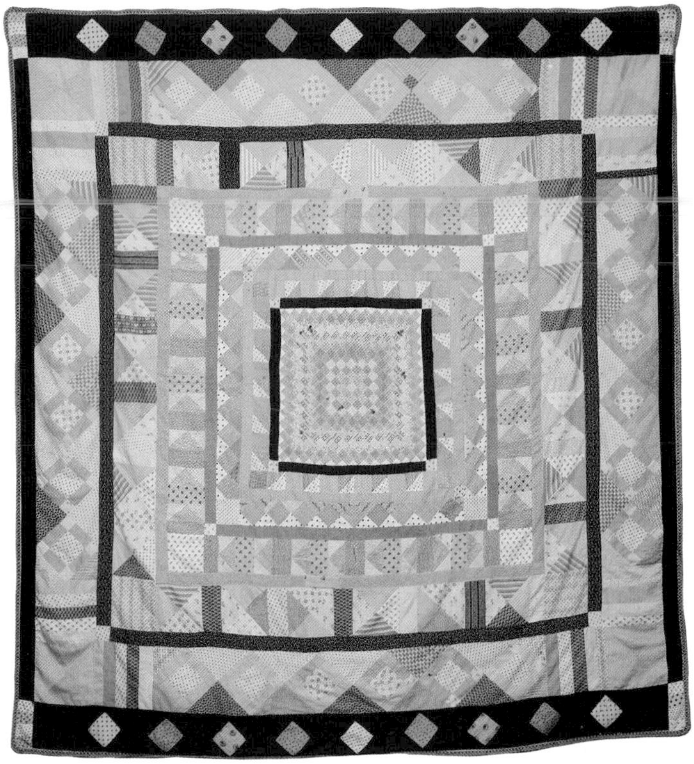

JAN TUDOR

Left: Log Cabin, *by Jeanette Dick, Sandhurst (Bendigo), 1867, 60 × 68 inches, pieced silks, velvets and satins, tied. The ruffle may have been added at a later date. Private collection. Right: Central Medallion, by Mary Ann Bruton, begun in Bendigo in 1873 and completed in Swan Hill in 1887, 91 × 110 inches, pieced cottons. Joined only by the binding. Collection of Marjorie Bruton, granddaughter of the quiltmaker.*

in Bendigo in 1873 and completed in Swan Hill in 1887 (this page). The design differs from the English style but remains a variation of a central medallion. Many Australian quilts of the late nineteenth century are similar to the Bruton patchwork. By contrast, in America by 1873 the central medallion design was no longer in use and the quilt of repeated blocks dominated.

Mary Ann Bruton (née Holley) was born in 1851 in Deloraine, Tasmania. Her mother had immigrated from Somerset, England, and had married in Deloraine in 1849. Mary Ann married a farmer, William Bruton, in Bendigo in 1868. She became the local dressmaker in the Bendigo district, and the small prints of cotton in the center of her quilt are leftover dressmaking scraps. She started the quilt in 1873, the year her second son was born, "patching the tiny pieces by hand whilst rocking his cradle with her foot."[22] The pieces in the center of the quilt (one-inch squares) date from this period. Life at that time was rough on the land in the Australian outback. There was no electricity, and the quilt was pieced by the light of a kerosene lamp. Mary Ann Bruton also sewed all the clothes for her family—she had eight children.

In 1885 the family moved to Swan Hill, as her husband had obtained a contract to carry goods by horse wagon between Swan Hill and Bendigo. Mary Ann did not complete her quilt until 1887. The materials outside the center medallion were purchased locally especially to finish the quilt and were pieced together by treadle machine.[23] The quilt was backed with a cotton print which was produced for Queen Victoria's jubilee in 1887 and printed with the rose, the shamrock and the thistle (the leek for Wales missing) together with a cameo of Queen Victoria. The finished quilt has no batting, nor is it quilted, but is simply held together by the binding. The quilt was first exhibited and won two first prizes at the Kerang District Agricultural Fair of 1888. It must have been considered an extraordinary piece of women's fancywork, because it won first prize for the next nine years, from 1889 through 1897.

(In later fairs, one could not exhibit any item more than once.)

Another quilt produced and exhibited in this period was made by Elizabeth Keen, a dressmaker of Fyansford, Geelong, Victoria (page 67). Elizabeth Keen (née Hooton) was born in 1832 in Lincolnshire, England, and married Joseph Wensor. They came to Australia in the 1850's and settled in Modewarre (near Fyansford). Here their six children were born (four survived), the youngest being Elizabeth (born 1860) and Christina (1862). In 1869 Joseph died, and Elizabeth, with two children under the age of nine, purchased and became licensee of the Junction Hotel, Fyansford. (It was considered respectable for a widow to own a hotel; an unmarried woman would have been ostracized for such activity.) She ran the hotel and also conducted the first Sunday School of Fyansford in the parlor of the hotel. In 1872 she married Charles Keen,

a farm laborer, who took over the seven-room hotel,[24] and this gave her the freedom to return to dressmaking, where she was known as an excellent needlewoman.

In 1879 the Geelong Industrial and Juvenile Exhibition was held. It is extremely likely that Elizabeth Keen made her quilt for this exhibition, as it is signed and dated "Mrs E. Keen, Junction Hotel, Fyansford, 1879." A new exhibition hall was erected in Market Square, and His Excellency the Marquis of Normandy opened the exhibition with much palaver and festivities. The *Geelong Advertiser* ran a special four-page supplement reporting the dinners, speeches, celebrations and the grandness of the new Exhibition Building.[25] Fifteen women were awarded prizes for patchwork quilts and Elizabeth Keen was awarded a silver medal as first prize for a crochet quilt.[26] Although her patchwork quilt ap-

pears folksy and charming to us today, perhaps it did not reflect the high standard of fine needlework required at that time for a prize. (The other exhibitions at that time, Sydney International, 1879, and Melbourne Juvenile and Industrial Exhibition, 1879, do not record an entry from Elizabeth Keen.) However, her quilt is one of the few surviving examples of an Australian nineteenth-century repeating block quilt (other than *Log Cabin* designs).

It was obviously fashionable for women to produce quilts during this period and highly desirable that ladies' work should be encouraged by regular exhibition, such as at agricultural fairs and international exhibitions, paralleling what was happening in England and America in the latter half of the nineteenth century. The International Exhibition held in Sydney in 1879 included a separate Ladies' Court which, amongst other fancywork, included needle-

A late-nineteenth-century photograph of Elizabeth Keen (center) and her daughters Elizabeth and Christina outside the Junction Hotel. Charles Keen is seated in the horse-drawn buggy. Collection of the Geelong Historical Records Center.

Unknown Pattern, by Elizabeth Keen, Junction Hotel, Fyansford, Geelong, c. 1879, 96 × 110 inches, pieced (using paper templates) and appliquéd cottons, silks, velvets and wools on canvas, decorated with embroidery and buttons. Signed and dated in cross-stitch. Collection of the Queenscliffe Historical Society, Queenscliffe, Victoria.

made more than one quilt. However, quilts were commonly made as wedding gifts and twenty-first birthday presents. The utilization of Australian patchwork was also more akin to English customs. Between 1830 and 1870, silk patchworks were used as tablecloths or throws. At the peak of the Victorian era, a conglomeration of patchwork tea cosies, nightgown sachets, doll quilts, patchwork dresses and dressing gowns was produced, as well as quilts with elaborate crocheted borders or silk fringes for decorative throws.

The crazy quilt came to Australia in the 1880's and 1890's and was made well into the 1930's, and instructions were published in Australian magazines.[29] An example of an Australian crazy quilt is one made by Minnie McLoughlin between 1885 and 1890 for her trousseau (page 68). However, she was jilted by her sailor fiancé and never married. By 1910 she was truly regarded as an "old maid" and gave the quilt to Elsie Whelan, the daughter of her best friend, as a wedding present. Minnie worked at Brownell's, a drapery store in Hobart, Tasmania, and the materials in the quilt are scraps she saved from the store.

There are many surviving crazy quilts from the period of 1880–1910 and many more recollections and memories of such quilts which no longer exist. Many of these quilts were made from scraps from wedding dresses, babies' ribbons and those collected by the maker from friends far and near. Australian flora and fauna are often represented on the quilts (such as wattle, emus, kangaroos), as are naval badges,

work. A patchwork quilt exhibited by Mrs. Hatton of Liverpool in this exhibition contained seven thousand pieces.[27] Fancywork sections were also included in other colonial international exhibitions, as well as at the Women's Industry Exhibition and Centenary Fair of 1888.[28]

The United States courts of the Australian International Exhibitions do not appear to have contained any patchwork, but the Australian courts of the Philadelphia 1876 Centennial Exposition and the 1893 Chicago World's Columbian Exposition contained possum and platypus-skin patch-

works made by the ladies of NSW. At the Sydney Intercolonial Exhibition of 1870, Mrs. Robertson of Glebe had two quilts for sale at 8 pounds 10 shillings and 5 pounds. As it cost 1 shilling to 2 shillings sixpence per night to stay at Elizabeth Keen's Junction Hotel, it is obvious that patchwork quilts were highly prized and expensive items.

Australian quilting and patchwork in the late nineteenth century did not involve the same social or community activity as in the United States. There is no evidence of quilting bees or album quilts. Few women seem to have

MARK BARKTEOVITCH

Crazy, by Minnie McLoughlin, Hobart, Tasmania, c. 1890, 80 × 85 inches, velvets and silks, with embroidery, tied. Collection of Beryl Brown.

together with quaint scripted morals and sayings. Many are signed and dated. Some are embellished with buttons, badges and ribbons. Some crazy quilts are stuffed so that each square or block is raised by a mass of padding.

During the Australian crazy-quilt period of the late nineteenth century, idiosyncratic quiltmaking began to appear, such as a quilt which re-affirmed Australia's current patriotism to England and Queen Victoria (this page). The quilt is composed of individual blocks of white embroidery on red Indian head-cloth of pictorial scenes depicting the life in the village of Westbury, Tasmania. The center block shows Queen Victoria in Elizabethan costume, and the surrounding blocks show the houses of Westbury, the farm animals (including an emu and a kangaroo) and a multitude of Victorian sayings, proverbs and tributes to the Empire.

By the late nineteenth century, Australia had acquired great wealth and there was a tremendous feeling of national identity, as over half the population were Australian-born. Australian symbols and motifs appeared on all forms of decorative art such as pottery, jewelry, furniture and architecture. In 1901, Federation occurred after a long political struggle and the separate colonies in Australia were joined into one nation—the Commonwealth of Australia. Although an Australian coat of arms was not officially granted until 1908, many earlier items of Australian decorative art incorporate the maker's own version of an Australian coat of arms.

One such example is the quilt which was found in the possession of the Swann sisters who lived at Elizabeth Farm (page 70). William Swann arrived in Sydney in 1864 and married Elizabeth Devlin in 1870. They had twelve children, nine girls and three boys (one of whom died in infancy) born between 1871 and 1898. The Swann family purchased Elizabeth Farm (the old Macarthur home) in 1904 when William became the headmaster at Parramatta North Superior Public School. He was a highly respected gentleman and there was scarcely

A detail of the center of a sampler quilt, by a member of the Hampson family, Westbury, Tasmania, c. 1900–1905, 69 × 88 inches, hand embroidery on Indian head-cloth. Joined on by the binding. The quilt was probably made for a raffle or contest; one block is inscribed "GOOD · LUCK · TO · THE · WINNER · OF · THIS". Collection of Genevieve Fitzpatrick.

any activity in the Parramatta district in which he was not involved. He encouraged all his daughters to have professional or semi-professional careers and was actively involved in the women's suffrage movement together with some of his daughters. When he died in 1909, he left behind his wife and eight unmarried daughters who lived till the end of their lives at Elizabeth Farm. Three of the Swann sisters became head-mistresses, two became music teachers, one ran a business college at Elizabeth Farm, one was a Sunday school teacher and another ran Elizabeth Farm as the housekeeper.

The Swann quilt is made from salesmen's samples and was found amongst family possessions in 1968. The central coat of arms has the emu and kangaroo posed outwards but looking inwards, whereas in the official version of 1908 both animals face inwards. The earliest medal with a similar coat of arms to the Swann quilt was struck in 1853, but the coat of arms on the Swann quilt, dated through numismatics, is most likely to be around 1890[30] (about the same time as the fight for Federation began). Margaret, the eldest sister (1871–1963), was the one member of the Swann family extremely interested in Australian history. She wrote many articles, amongst which is a history of Elizabeth Macarthur.[31] Knowing of Margaret's keen interest in the history of her country, Mrs. Brown of Bowning, a friend of the family, made the quilt and presented it to Margaret.

Australia in the nineteenth century produced a rich heritage of old patchwork quilts. Many of the quilts discovered to date come from the colder states (Tasmania and Victoria), and yet very few of the quilts contain batting and, hence, few of the patchwork items are quilted. As Macarthur brought wool to Australia at the very beginning of the colony, and wool blankets served as bedding through the nineteenth century, it appears that

An 1893 photograph of the Swann family, from left to right, back row: Mary, Priscilla, Rebecca, Elizabeth and Margaret; center row: Isabella, William holding Ruth, Elizabeth holding Frederic; front row: John (on tricycle), Edith and William. Courtesy of Elizabeth Plimer (née Swann).

quilts were made purely as a decorative art to be admired in the home or exhibited at agricultural fairs and exhibitions. The story alters in the early twentieth century, as quilts became a salvage art and were regarded as utilitarian items.

It is probable that in early Australia only the ladies of the upper or middle classes could afford the luxury or time to produce patchwork quilts, and perhaps this is exemplified by the predominance of central medallion quilts which required a large work space to complete and copied the prevalent style of the English manor houses of the time. There appear to be few quilts from the convict or lower classes, but again, perhaps these have not survived. It also appears that many of the quilts made throughout the century were produced by dressmakers or women who had ready access to fabrics and who would have been middle-class women.

The early colonial quilts of Australia resemble late-eighteenth-century and early-nineteenth-century English quilts and the early colonial quilts of America. However, Australian quilts continued to be made in a central medallion style until the arrival of the crazy quilt, while in America the medallion quilt had all but disappeared by the 1870's and the repeating block was used to create larger secondary designs. Except for the *Log Cabin,* which is very common, it appears that very few repeating block quilts of this type were made in Australia until the twentieth century.

Although only a handful of nineteenth-century Australian quilts have been selected here to portray the nature of Australian women's lives and the influence of the social and technological changes from convict times to Commonwealth, many hundreds of nineteenth-century quilts have been discovered and documented over the past five years. We are beginning to discover that Australia has a rich quiltmaking heritage and are paying tribute to the women of our past for their expressive form of needlework which has been passed down to us through the generations.

Central Medallion, by Mrs. Brown of Bowning for Margaret Swann of Elizabeth Farm, Parramatta, c. 1890–1900, 72 × 90 inches, pieced and appliquéd cottons. Collection of Leigh Taumoefolau.

LEIGH ATKINSON

REFERENCE LIST

1. Thomas Timpson, *Memoirs of Mrs. Elizabeth Fry* (New York: Stanford and Swords, 1847), pp. 116–117.

2. Marsden Files, State Library of New South Wales, Ms. A1992, pp. 224–226.

3. Jane Whitney, *Elizabeth Fry, Quaker Heroine* (London: George G. Harrap and Co., Ltd., 1937), p. 170.

4. G. B. Barton, *History of New South Wales from the Records* (Sydney: Charles Potter, Government Printer, 1889), pp. 449–450.

5. British Parliamentary Papers 1838, Q-210-26, quoted in Beverley Kingston, *The World Moves Slowly: A Documentary History of Australian Women* (Stanmore, NSW: Cassell, 1977), pp. 22-23.

6. Whitney, p. 160.

7. Anne McMahon, "The Lady in Early Colonial Society," *Papers and Proceedings of the Tasmanian Historical Research Association*, XXVI, no. 1 (1979), 5-14.

8. Anne Summers, "Factory Girls, Refractory Girls," *Refractory Girl*, Summer 1972-1973, pp. 15-17.

9. Ruth Teale, *Colonial Eve: Sources of Women in Australia 1788-1914* (Melbourne: Oxford University Press, 1978), pp. 38-64.

10. Teale, pp. 64-73.

11. Macarthur Papers, State Library of New South Wales, Ms. A2906, quoted in Hazel King, *Elizabeth Macarthur and Her World* (Sydney: Sydney University Press, 1980), pp. 11-14.

12. Susan Hunt, "Restoring Elizabeth Farm: Colonial Textiles," *Craft Australia*, II (1985), 81-88. Many ledger entries by John Macarthur record the purchase of fabrics and soft furnishings. In one purchase he spent ninety-two pounds on material alone, but he also imported fabric for resale. The border of the quilt, which is crochet, may have been added at a later time.

13. Florence M. Montgomery, *Printed Textiles, English and American Cottons and Linens, 1700-1850* (New York: The Viking Press, 1970), pp. 141, 144, 152, 156, 159, 162-163, 356.

14. See, for example, the quilts in the Charleston (South Carolina) Museum collection, in Lacy Folmar Bullard, "The Collector: Once Out of Time," *The Quilt Digest 3*, pp. 8-21.

15. Morton Herman, *Annabella Boswell's Journal* (Sydney: Angus and Robertson, 1981), pp. 89-90.

16. Teale, p. 72.

17. The silk *Tumbling Blocks* quilts are perhaps the most commonly found old quilts in Australia. Many were made with paper templates (some with dates and locations on the papers) right up to the 1890's. Obviously, the hexagon quilts made by the same technique were also very popular.

18. Barbara Brackman, "A Chronological Index to Pieced Quilt Patterns, 1775-1825," *Uncoverings 1983*, ed. by Sally Garoutte (Mill Valley, Calif.: American Quilt Study Group, 1984), p. 106.

19. *Ballarat Times*, September 2, 1854 and October 28, 1854.

20. Last Will and Testament of Hugh Livingston, 1862, in the possession of Margaret Anne Thomas.

21. It is interesting to conjecture whether the Americans arriving at the gold rush may have brought with them the *Log Cabin* design. The census of April 26, 1854 reports that 2,761 persons born in the United States were living in Victoria. However, they were far outnumbered by the immigrants from England, Scotland and Ireland, so the chances are higher that the pattern came to Australia from there.

22. Letter to the author from Marjorie Bruton, January 30, 1985.

23. The sewing machine was imported from America during the gold rush, as were the American-style covered wagon produced by Australia's Cobb & Co., the stove, the wooden wash tub and the ice chest, all of which brought the American influence directly into the Australian home. See L. G. Churchwood, *Australia and America 1788-1972: An Alternative History* (Chippendale, Sydney: Alternative Publishing Cooperative Ltd., 1979), pp. 60, 66.

24. *Geelong Advertiser*, June 8, 1879.

25. *Geelong Advertiser*, December 19, 1879.

26. Edward Hurst, *Official List of Awards, Geelong Industrial and Juvenile Exhibition 1879-80* (Geelong: Henry Ranks, 1879), pp. 6-9.

27. *Report of the Sydney International Exhibition* (Sydney: Government Printer, 1881), p. 517.

28. During the second half of the nineteenth century there were three levels of exhibitions held in Australia: international exhibitions such as the 1879 Sydney International Exhibition, 1880 Melbourne International Exhibition and 1888 Centennial Melbourne Exhibition; intercolonial exhibitions; agricultural local exhibitions such as the Kerang District Agricultural Fair. Both the international and intercolonial exhibitions were largely trade fairs, although they often included educational displays of fine and applied arts. The international exhibition of 1879 in Sydney lists six Australian patchwork quilts (approximately five per cent of the total fancywork entries) which were awarded medals in addition to one from Great Britain, and the 1888 Centennial Melbourne Exhibition also lists six winning patchwork quilts. By contrast, the Melbourne Intercolonial Juvenile and Industrial Exhibition of 1879 lists thirty-one patchwork quilts (one containing three thousand pieces which was made by twenty schoolchildren), and the number exhibited in local agricultural fairs was much greater.

29. Lance Rawson, *Australian Enquiry Book of Household and General Information* (Sydney: Kangaroo Press, 1894), pp. 126, 128-129.

30. L. J. Carlisle, *Australian Commemorative Medals and Medalets from 1788* (Sydney: B and C Press Pty. Ltd., 1983), pp. 5-69.

31. Margaret Swann, "Elizabeth Macarthur," *Journal and Proceedings of the Parramatta and District Historical Society*, III (1926), 147-157.

ANNETTE GERO is one of Australia's first quilt historians. She has published widely and lectures frequently on the history of old quilts. Recently she was elected a Fellow of the Royal Society of Arts (London) for her contribution to historical quilt research. A collector of antique quilts, her collection was exhibited in Sydney last year.

Professionally she has a doctorate in biochemistry and works at the University of New South Wales in Sydney.

The author would particularly like to thank the owners of the quilts already acknowledged in the text and the following people whose knowledge and enthusiasm have contributed greatly to the writing of this article: Professor Beverley Kingston, Professor of History, University of NSW; Dr. James Broadbent, Curator, Rouse Hill; Susan Hunt, Curator, Elizabeth Farm; Rhonda Hamilton and Glenda King, Queen Victoria Museum and Art Gallery; Ray Raison, the Queenscliffe Historical Society; Norman Houghton, Archivist, Geelong Historical Research Center; Michael Bogle, editor, Craft Australia; and special thanks to Les Carlisle, Patricia McDonald, Wendy Holland, Graham Whale and Fay Sudweeks.

Eagle, c. 1880–1910, Cherrytree, Pennsylvania, 73½ × 77 inches, appliquéd cottons.

SOMETHING OLD

When, as a college student, I began buying antique quilts in the late 1960's, I was unaware that across North America quiltmakers and artists were continuing the tradition of making large quilts from small bits and pieces of cloth. I knew that my mother had made a quilt when she was a girl, being taught by my seamstress grandmother to piece and quilt. And I was the proud owner of quilts made by grandmothers and great-aunts from both sides of my family. But in those days it never entered my mind that there might be living quiltmakers creating quilts—quilts that I would admire and enjoy. I was caught up in buying the old ones, standing under a tree in an auction yard for most of an afternoon to get the chance to bid five dollars on a scrap-bag quilt that I'd take back to school to brighten up an otherwise stark college room.

Even in the 1970's, as my interest in quilts grew and I began to buy more of them, developing into an antique-quilt dealer, I did not realize what was going on around me: hundreds of thousands of women were sewing and making quilts. I was still caught up in the magic of finding and buying quilts from our past.

In retrospect, my belated realization of what was happening around me is typical of most antique-

BY MICHAEL KILE

#25, by Pamela Studstill, Pipe Creek, Texas, 1983, 58 x 59 inches, machine-pieced and hand-quilted cottons painted by hand.

SOMETHING NEW

quilt lovers and collectors. To this day, the vast majority of antique-quilt collectors have not "discovered" today's glorious quilts. It is as if, like early sea voyagers, they fear that they will fall off the end of the quilt world if they venture beyond that posted, arbitrary warning marked "c. 1940." They have yet to make the comforting discovery that quilt-making, like all creative pursuits, is a continuum.

The antique-quilt collector's preoccupation is, of course, understandable. During the past twenty years, most North Americans have looked to their past with nostalgic longings. The past's horrors have been forgotten in an almost frenzied attempt to romanticize the so-called halcyon days of grueling travel cross-continent in an ox cart, famines and plagues and the back-breaking, dawn-to-dark toil of field work. Far more beautiful than the times in which they were made, antique quilts have been popularized as symbols of a past which has been misrepresented as easier and better than our own. But the old quilts lift our spirits in an age in which we question our very priorities. They remind us of a time in which the need to scratch out a living, to survive, placed everything else in an understandable perspective. In our desire to acknowledge quilts as exemplary of the best from our past, we lost

Log Cabin variation, c. 1875–1910, York County, Pennsylvania, 74 x 89½ inches, wools.

sight of the fact that we should also be chroniclers of our present.

There are, however, signs that some collectors are looking beyond 1940, into the present, and defying the diehard antiquarians who persist in denigrating today's quilts with hackneyed criticisms like "They just don't make them like they used to." After all, it doesn't take many visits to exhibitions displaying traditional and contemporary designs by living quiltmakers to realize that the fine work of the past has been preserved—and extended—by today's accomplished practitioners.

In 1984 I started getting telephone calls from quiltmakers around the world. They all asked the same question: "Who are Ardis and Robert James?" Many of these needleworkers are now familiar with this quilt-collecting couple, as are several discriminating quilt dealers, for the Jameses are rare collectors, ones whose passion for quilts has broken the bounds normally associated with quilt collecting: they enthusiastically collect modern as well as antique quilts.

Entering the James home, one need not ask what they collect. Hanging from every wall possible, displayed on beds and arranged on racks throughout their New England-style house, are quilts. Here is an early-fabric quilt, there is a dazzling Pennsylvania appliqué and around the corner in the staircase hangs a new work by English quiltmaker Pauline Burbidge. Old is mixed with new, appliquéd is shown next to pieced, in a random arrangement that announces the owners' preoccupation: these people have caught the quilt-collecting bug, pure and simple.

Ardis bought their first quilt in 1978 at "Quilts: An American Romance" in Troy, Michigan. "I didn't intend to buy a quilt," she says, "but I saw this huge *Mariner's Compass*. It had a hole in it, but it was gorgeous; it was big and it had a border on it the likes of which I haven't seen since. I paid one hundred dollars for it, and that was a lot of money. After I purchased it, a dealer walked up to me and said, 'Oh, you're the one that bought that quilt. I used to own that quilt. In fact, everybody has owned that quilt!' " Ardis pauses, then adds, "She didn't bother me a bit."

Although he wasn't thrilled about its condition, Robert liked the quilt, too. So, the next year at Troy, Ardis bought two quilts. The following year—six. "I was a little nervous that year," she admits. "We hadn't actually said that we were going to collect quilts, but when I got home Bob asked, 'Did you buy any quilts?' I answered, 'Yes, six.' 'Great,' he said. He liked everything I bought. So, the next year I went to Troy and Bob called me from home and asked, 'Are you buying quilts?' I answered, 'Yes, I bought a few.' And he said, 'That's great.' So I thought, 'If it takes so little to make this man happy, I'm going to give him a real thrill.' And I bought sixteen!"

Ardis had already started making her own first quilt (a blue-and-white sampler) when she bought their first antique quilt. She spent two years making her quilt. She had seen a similar quilt at a quilt-guild exhibition in her area and was so struck by it she decided she had to make one herself. She had been a partner in a fabric shop with three other women friends. They started the shop in 1964 and she remained a partner for nine years. Says Ardis, "I had done all the other things: the volunteer work, the PTA, the Scouts. It was time to do something else." Before making her sampler quilt, Ardis had sewn for years, but her work had always involved clothes that she could wear. She had never even considered quiltmaking. "That blue-and-white sampler quilt changed my life."

For five years, the Jameses bought antique quilts until, in 1983, they purchased their first contemporary quilts from Michael James (no relation), from whom Ardis had taken quiltmaking workshops. Those purchases made them realize that there was no reason for them to confine their collecting to older quilts. Today, they own over one hundred antique pieces and fifty contemporary ones. And they are quick to add that they feel as if they have just started their contemporary purchases. "So far," says Ardis, "we have quilts by more than a dozen contemporary quiltmakers. We have works by Sonya Lee Barrington, Caryl Fallert, Françoise Barnes, Chris Wolf Edmonds, Virginia Avery, and several quilts each by Jean Ray Laury, Pauline Burbidge, Pamela Studstill and Michael James."

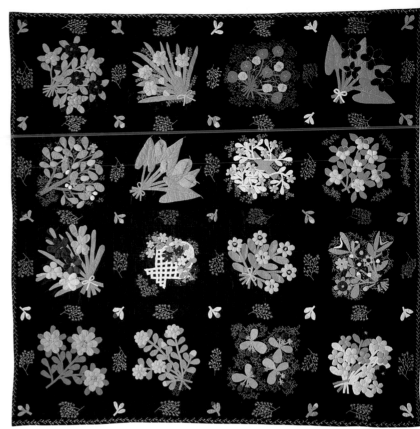

Album, c. 1880–1900, eastern Pennsylvania, 86 ½ × 87 inches, appliquéd silks and satins, with padding, embroidery and three-dimensional projections.

Hen Quilt I, by Pauline Burbidge, Nottingham, England, 1986, 42 × 49 inches, appliquéd and pieced cottons, some hand-dyed. Zig-zag and straight machine stitching decorates the surface. Machine-quilted with an industrial multi-needle quilting machine.

With literally hundreds of thousands of potential quiltmakers to choose from, one could ask why they have more than one quilt by any quiltmaker. "That's easy," responds Robert. "First of all, there are lots of people on our lists for future purchases, but we also feel that one quilt cannot possibly represent a quiltmaker's work. One quilt doesn't tell you a whole heck of a lot about an artist. As a collector, you must show how an artist has changed and progressed. That's very important. And that makes collecting contemporary quilts very different from buying old ones. One rarely has the chance to identify, let alone purchase, more than one quilt by a deceased quiltmaker. But building a collection of contemporary art quilts is far more complex than collecting antique ones. In antique quilts, there's an established market. One knows within what price range a mint condition Amish *Diamond in the Square* should fit. With contemporary quilts, the market is brand new; you're on your own. But it's a heck of a lot of fun." They both talk openly of a massive expansion of their contemporary-quilt collecting. Adds Ardis, "I don't understand why there aren't more people collecting antique *and* contemporary quilts. How can you have one without the other?"

Unlike his wife, Robert James doesn't sew, but his mother and grandmothers did. Raised in Nebraska, like Ardis, Robert remembers sitting under his mother's quilting frame, listening to her and her friends talking while they quilted. "I liked hiding under that frame, watching the needles glide in and out of the fabric," he reminisces. Their close ties to quiltmaking and sewing have obviously influenced their collecting passion. And their familiarity with the medium has allowed them to relax and enjoy their collecting in ways one does not often see among collectors. They have allowed their collection to evolve, with little monitoring; they have not set specific goals (beyond the desire to see their collection grow), and they are more than satisfied that they have never sat down and tried to analyze their acquisitions. For example, Ardis maintains that she is far more attracted to pieced quilts than appliqués, and yet exceptional appliqués are among

Turkey Tracks or **Wandering Foot**, c. 1850–1865, Randolph County, Indiana, 71 x 79 inches, pieced and appliquéd cottons, with trapunto. Signed "E. E. McNary" in embroidery.

their finest holdings. "I guess our way of collecting isn't the best way," says Ardis, "but I'll get around to doing a better job of collecting once I get all the quilts I like."

Talking about their collecting habits, the Jameses come alive. "Buying a quilt is a very emotional experience for me," says Ardis. "I make up my mind in about five seconds." Robert smiles. "Well, maybe not *five* seconds," he says, but quickly adds, "but she's darned fast. We buy from dealers we know and trust. We're not the types to go around from dealer to dealer, show to show. That's a very poor use of your time. You have to look through a lot of junk before you find what you're after. It's a lot better (at least it has been for us) to pick your dealers and have them come to you with what they think will appeal to you. Dealers aren't dumb. They know they can't afford to treat us badly. We're good buyers. So, they do a lot of our leg work and it's well worthwhile to pay them for that effort. Besides, if you pick your dealers well, they're going to know a lot more about the field than you do." Adds Ardis, "It's really quite simple: we went around looking at quilts, found the best ones and met the dealers who had them. From there, we picked whom we wanted to do business with. It wasn't very hard at all."

The Jameses' collection represents a broad cross-section of American quiltmaking. Among the antique and contemporary works they possess are appliqués and pieced works, crazies and *Log Cabin* quilts. And there are Amish, works composed of early fabrics and quilts with heavy trapunto. And yet it is not this wide variety of quilt styles and types that catches one's eye. It is the whimsy and individualistic character of virtually every quilt in their collection that pierces one's consciousness. This is a collection with quirks and abounding personality. The quilts in it were chosen without premeditation; they are truly reflections of their current owners. One has the distinct impression that the Jameses would enjoy having dinner with the makers of all their quilts—and that the makers would be equally pleased at the prospect. Thus, the Jameses do not own a plain *Basket* quilt or plainly composed *Eagle* quilt, but ones like those pictured in these pages. The Jameses are seekers of the uncommon. "Who wants a simple collection?" asks Ardis. One senses she would dare her guest to answer affirmatively. "I

Basket, c. 1870–1900, origin unknown, 83 × 102 inches, pieced and appliquéd cottons.

here to build a field, to work with others to build a collecting field that includes all types of quilts. That should be a lot of fun."

True to their enthusiasms, the Jameses have decided to take a step most collectors haven't even considered: they have had architectural plans drawn up for an addition to their home. They plan to build their own quilt museum, an area that will be devoted exclusively to the display and care of their collection. Watching them sitting over their plans, talking animatedly to each other, one knows that they regard this step in their collecting careers as an important but natural one; for them, it seems only logical to be making plans to build a home for their quilts, quilts for which their adult daughter and son—both quilt enthusiasts in the making—will someday be the custodians.

By their very activity and focus, the Jameses are proclaiming a new vision for quilt collectors that encompasses all of quiltmaking. With a devotion to the quilt medium—as evidenced by those architectural plans—they are challenging their fellow aficionados to join them in giving emphasis to both the past and the present.

want a collection that's devious, one that attracts people from many different vantage points, for a variety of reasons. I like all quilts. I have never met a quilt in which I couldn't find something to like."

As collectors, the Jameses started late; most of the major collections in America were begun before the late 1970's, but that doesn't dampen the Jameses' enthusiasm. Revealing his business background, Robert adds, "The worst thing you can do is try to get in at the bottom of a market. Who can judge that? Just begin." Because they had a family to raise and children to educate, the Jameses' collection has been put together from a budget that before 1978 was allocated to college educations and, Robert adds, "new cars every other year. Everybody has to operate on a budget, but any middle-income couple has the ability, if they want to make changes in their spending patterns, to surround themselves with a number of very nice quilts. But besides the sheer enjoyment we both receive from collecting quilts, there's another excitement for me. We have a chance

Princess Feather variation, c. 1880–1910, York County (Pennsylvania) Mennonite, 84 × 84 inches, appliquéd cottons.

The *Quilt Digest*
series. Collect each
volume in this annual
series which highlights
exceptional antique
and contemporary
quilts and the writings
of the world's fore-
most quilt experts. By
doing so, you will as-
semble an up-to-date,
authoritative encyclo-
pedia of quilt informa-
tion and photographs.
There is nothing like
The Quilt Digest.

Other Books from...

◄ *The Quilt Digest 5.* Extraordinary quilts from around the world, plus a portrait of six international quiltmakers, an exploration of how quilts unite the generations, unusual antique quilts made from fabrics issued by tobacco companies, the first comprehensive presentation of antique Australian quilts, a look at a trailblazing collection of antique and contemporary quilts. 80 pages. 78 color photographs. $16.95.

1. *The Quilt Digest 1.* Remarkable quilts, plus Michael James interview, *Log Cabin* quilts, Amish home interiors, a Jewish immigrant's quilt, the Esprit Amish collection, quilt documentation techniques. 72 pages. 52 color and 18 black-and-white photographs. $14.95.

2. *The Quilt Digest 2.* Many rare quilts, plus a superb private collection, vintage photos of crazy quilts in a Victorian home, a pioneer wife and her quilt, quilt care and conservation, Hawaiian Flag quilts. 80 pages. 60 color photographs and 17 black-and-white photographs and illustrations. $14.95.

3. *The Quilt Digest 3.* Dozens of exceptional quilts, plus Quaker quilts, formal Southern quilts from the Charleston (South Carolina) Museum collection, a short story about a wife and husband and their quilt, eccentric quilts, an Alabama pioneer and her quilts. 88 pages. 93 color photographs. $15.95.

4. *The Quilt Digest 4.* A variety of exceptional quilts, plus *Pine Tree* quilts, a black, self-help quilting co-operative, a nineteenth-century "old maid" and the quilt made for her by her quilting-bee friends, quilts in modern art, a quilt dealer's private collection. 88 pages. 75 color and 8 black-and-white photographs. $16.95.

5. *The Adventures of Sunbonnet Sue.* Internationally known quiltmaker Jean Ray Laury has plucked familiar Sunbonnet Sue off the tranquil surface of her quilt and plunged her into the turbulent everyday life of a harried wife and mother. As a quilt enthusiast, you will appreciate Sue's awe-inspiring adventures: you may even recognize many of them as your own as you giggle, then guffaw your way through this hilarious cartoon series. All drawings by the author. 24 pages each. $4.95 each.

6. *Homage to Amanda* by Edwin Binney, 3rd and Gail Binney-Winslow. A great quilt collection bountifully illustrates this concise guide to the first two hundred years of American quiltmaking. Published by Roderick Kiracofe/ R K Press and distributed exclusively by The Quilt Digest Press. 96 pages. 71 color photographs. $18.95.

THE QUILT DIGEST PRESS

Hearts and Hands: The Influence of Women & Quilts on American Society by Pat Ferrero, Elaine Hedges and Julie Silber. Within the stunning, photograph-laden pages of this book is revealed the important role played by women and quilts in the last century's great movements and events—industrialization, the abolition of slavery, the Civil War, the westward expansion and pioneer experience, temperance and suffrage. Once you have read this extraordinary book, you will never forget it. 112 pages. 53 color and 39 black-and-white photographs. $19.95 paperback. $29.95 hard cover. ▼

7. *The Art Quilt* by Penny McMorris and Michael Kile. Quilts made by sixteen leading quiltmakers especially for this landmark book are the focus of a fascinating, in-depth look at this century's quiltmaking movement and the emergence of the contemporary quilt. A remarkable achievement. 136 pages. 79 color and 8 black-and-white photographs. $21.95 paperback. $29.95 hard cover. $10.00 fine-art poster.

8. *Remember Me: Women & Their Friendship Quilts* by Linda Otto Lipsett. A thorough examination of friendship quilts and an intimate portrait of seven nineteenth-century quiltmakers who made them, rendered in astonishing detail. A uniquely personal book that will transport you back into an earlier time. 136 pages. 112 color and 23 black-and-white photographs. $19.95 paperback. $29.95 hard cover.

Ordering Information. Thousands of quilt, antique, book and museum shops around the world carry the books and posters we publish. Check with shops in your area. Or you may order directly from us.

To order, send us your name, address, city, state and zip code. Tell us which books or posters you wish to order and in what quantity. California residents add 6½% sales tax. Finally, to the price of the books or posters you order, add $1.75 for the first book or poster—or any number of Sunbonnet Sue books—and $1.00 for each additional book or poster to cover postage and handling charges. Enclose your check made payable to *The Quilt Digest Press* and mail it, along with the above information, to Dept. D, 955 Fourteenth Street, San Francisco 94114.

Readers outside North America may have their orders shipped via air mail by including $8.00 for each book or poster—or Sunbonnet Sue set—ordered. All orders must be accompanied by payment in U.S. dollars drawn on a U.S. bank.

Depending upon the season of the year, allow 4–6 weeks for delivery. Readers outside North America should allow several additional weeks for sea delivery.

We are happy to send gift books or posters directly to recipients.

Wholesale information is available to retailers upon request.

Our Mailing List. If your name is not on our mailing list and you would like it to be, please write to us. We will be happy to add your name so that you will receive advance information about our forthcoming books.